Day by Day with God

September–December 1998

Day by Day With God

Bible Readings for Women

SEPTEMBER–DECEMBER 1998

Christina Press
Bible Reading Fellowship
Crowborough/Oxford

Copyright © 1998 Christina Press and BRF

BRF, Peter's Way, Sandy Lane West, Oxford, OX4 5HG

First published in Great Britain 1998

ISBN 1 84101 008 1

Jacket design: Bookprint Creative Services Eastbourne

Trade representation in UK:
Kingsway Communications, Lottbridge Drove,
Eastbourne, East Sussex, BN23 6NT

Distributed in Australia by:
Hodder Headline Australia, 10–16 South Street,
Rydalmere, (Locked Bag 386), NSW 2116

Distributed in New Zealand by:
Scripture Union Wholesale, PO Box 760, Wellington

Distributed in South Africa by:
Struik Book Distributors, PO Box 193, Maitland 7405

Acknowledgments
Good News Bible copyright © American Bible Society
1966, 1971 and 1976, published by the Bible Societies
and Collins.

The Living Bible copyright © 1971 by Tyndale House
Publishers

The New Jerusalem Bible copyright © 1985 by Darton,
Longman & Todd Ltd and Doubleday & Company, Inc.

The Revised Standard Version of the Bible, copyright ©
1946, 1952, 1971 by the Division of Christian Education
of the National Council of the Churches of Christ in the
USA.

The Holy Bible, New International Version, copyright ©
1973, 1978, 1984 by International Bible Society. Used
by permission of Hodder & Stoughton Ltd.

New English Bible copyright © 1970 by permission of
Oxford and Cambridge University Presses.

Printed in Great Britain
by Caledonian Book Manufacturing International,
Glasgow

Contents

6	The Editor writes…	
8	Contributors	
10	A Morning Prayer	
11	His healing touch *Bridget Plass*	1–5 September
16	Romans 6 *Diana Archer*	6–12 September
23	Romans 8 *Hilary McDowell*	13–19 September
30	Solitude and silence *Alie Stibbe*	20 September–3 October
44	Psalms *Anne Coomes*	4–17 October
58	Luke 1 *Christina Rees*	18–31 October
72	Peace *Christine Leonard*	1–7 November
79	Remembrance Sunday	8 November
80	People who met Jesus *Rosemary Green*	9–21 November
93	Joy *Mary Reid*	22–28 November
100	Romans 12 *Jennifer Rees Larcombe*	29 November–12 December
114	Isaiah 11 *Elaine Pountney*	13–21 December
123	On Christmas… *Bridget Plass*	22–31 December
133	Magazine section	
156	Order forms	
158	Subscription information	

The Editor writes...

The summer holidays are over, and whichever way you look there is a sense of busyness. Children and teachers are busy getting to know their new year groups; farmers are working all hours to get the harvest in before the weather breaks. The squirrel at the bottom of the garden seems to epitomize the mood of the season, frantically burying hazelnuts in the lawn, preparing for the winter. I sit down with my diary and my husband's diary and start filling in entries to the end of the year and fuss because I haven't yet got a refill for 1999.

Just not enough time...
Busyness seems to be the state most of us find ourselves in. I have just been talking to one of our writers on the phone who was apologizing for a delay in getting her notes to me: 'But life has been so impossibly busy! I enjoy it all,' she went on, 'but there just isn't enough time.' Learning to deal with the over-busyness of our lives is a theme that comes over from most of our writers throughout the next four months. This wasn't planned or intended, it has just happened—so maybe this is something God wants to say to all of us as we rush through life. Hilary McDowell writes, 'How could his (Jesus') gentle, loving voice of mercy be heard above the deafening roar of her timetable, the daily demands of routine?'

So how do we keep 'keyed in' to the gentle voice of Jesus in the rush of the everyday? Jennifer Rees Larcombe takes us through some of the teaching of Paul from Romans 12, and she says how impossible she used to find the instruction to 'pray without ceasing' when she had six children to look after! She has found that it *is* possible, in our modern world, to be prayerful always, to be aware that Jesus is with her in every situation. We each need to find our own way of staying in the presence of Jesus throughout the day. I find it helpful, first thing in the morning, to look out of the window at the garden, the trees and the sky—all his creation—and commit whatever the new day holds to my heavenly Father. There is a short prayer on page 10 which you could use to key in to God at the beginning of each day.

The right perspective

And, of course, the whole purpose of *Day by Day with God* is just that: to help us realize that he is with us every day and all day. Alie Stibbe, with four children—the youngest a lively two-year-old—lives in a busy vicarage and felt she wanted to write notes on solitude and silence. I often feel depressed and glum as winter approaches and the days get shorter, so I have spent time looking at what the Bible says about joy. Christine Leonard, a new writer to join our team, has written notes on peace, because she is a worrier! Whatever situation or mood that we find ourselves in, there is something written in the Bible, somewhere, that will help us put everything into the right perspective—God's perspective. All of us who have contributed to this edition of *Day by Day with God* have tried to apply God's word to our daily lives, to help us see past the cares and trials of our uncertain world to the certainty of a loving heavenly Father who is always with us and who has a purpose for us.

Mary Reid

Contributors

Diana Archer has three young children and a degree in religious studies, and has served in Japan as a missionary. She has worked in the publishing world as a freelance editor and writer. Her book *Who'd Plant a Church?* was published in January.

Anne Coomes has been a journalist for the Church of England for nearly twenty years, including seven years as press officer for the Bishop of Peterborough. She currently works part-time for the Diocese of Chester and is writing her fifth book. She holds a degree in theology, and is a Reader-in-training for her parish.

Rosemary Green has an international speaking ministry, sometimes alongside her husband Michael. Her highly praised book *God's Catalyst*, now reprinted, distils her wisdom and experience gained through many years of prayer counselling. She is on the team of Springboard, the Archbishops' Initiative for Evangelism, and has recently returned to Oxford.

Margaret Killingray is a tutor at the Institute for Contemporary Christianity in London. She has assisted Dr John Stott and others in running Christian Impact conferences here and overseas, and is currently writing a book on Christian ethics. Margaret and her husband, David, have three daughters and four grandchildren.

Jennifer Rees Larcombe, one of Britain's best-loved Christian authors and speakers, lives in Kent. She writes from a recent experience of walking in the shadows. In recent years she has published a novel, the *Children's Bible Story Book*, and an account of her dramatic recovery, *Unexpected Healing*.

Christine Leonard lives in Surrey with her husband and two teenage children. She writes books for both adults and children; most tell the true stories of ordinary Christians who have done extraordinary things. She serves as Development Officer for the Association of Christian Writers.

Hilary McDowell is a deaconess in Belfast with a ministry of reconciliation and outreach through poetry, art, drama and music. Her book *Some Day I'm Going to Fly*, with a foreword by Adrian Plass, has made her name known internationally.

Bridget Plass studied at drama school and is a sought-after speaker who, when the family commitments permit, often travels with her husband Adrian. Her book *The Apple of His Eye* made its way into the top twenty Christian titles in 1997. But life, as she confesses, is not always lived at the top.

Elaine Pountney is a dynamic speaker and lecturer and a professional counsellor. Her home is in Toronto where her husband is Principal of Wycliffe, an Anglican theological college.

Christina Rees was born in America and spent her childhood travelling aboard a small wooden sailboat. She came to live in England twenty years ago when she met and married Chris Rees. She is a freelance writer and broadcaster, speaker, preacher and a member of the General Synod of the Church of England. She is also the Chair of WATCH (Women and the Church), a national organization that provides a forum for promoting women in the Church.

Mary Reid is the Editor of *Day by Day with God*. She is a trained teacher and a former magazine and book editor. She continues to be involved in education and is the special needs co-ordinator at a small village school and governor of another school. Her husband, Gavin, is now Bishop of Maidstone; they have two sons, a daughter and three grandchildren.

Alie Stibbe has contributed to *Renewal* and other Christian publications. She lives at St Andrew's Vicarage, Chorleywood, where her husband Mark is the vicar. Previously they ministered in Sheffield. Samuel, the youngest of their four children, is two years old.

Contributors are identified by their initials at the bottom of each page.

A Morning Prayer

Thank you, heavenly Father,
for this new day.
Be with me now
in all I do
and think
and say,
that it will be to your glory.

Amen

TUESDAY 1 SEPTEMBER   Luke 5:12–14 (RSV)

His healing touch

[Jesus] stretched out his hand and touched him...

Princess Diana and Mother Teresa were both prepared to touch the untouchable. I am not suggesting for a minute that Diana's work equalled the sacrificial lifestyle of Mother Teresa, but she showed remarkable commitment to the isolated, the weak and the rejected. Like Mother Teresa, she was prepared to enter worlds we have allowed ourselves to forget.

The other thing they had in common was their concentration on the individual. Mother Teresa, in her commitment to 'doing something beautiful for God', eased the last weeks and days of thousands of beggars dying on the streets of Calcutta, and through this brought not only their plight but that of the rejected in all societies to our notice. She taught us an amazing truth—that Jesus can be seen in those who need our care. But she did not sort out the whole problem of poverty in India.

Diana reached millions of people who desperately needed someone of value in the world to value *them*—to look into their eyes as if they were the most important people in the universe. Her memorial fund will go a long way towards eliminating the use of landmines, but she did not, of course, solve the problem of Aids.

Caring for the individual was always the Jesus way. It is behind World Vision, TEARFUND and Christian Aid and is central to the way he worked.

Jesus' very being, God made man, brought healing to those he met. His parables were told in order that people might turn and be healed. His occasional anger highlighted wrongdoing in order that people might be restored. The trust he placed in followers was lifegiving. He could have cured all illness for ever, thereby eradicating most taboos, but he didn't. He dealt individually with each situation, and by this method chose to highlight the cruelty of those taboos.

Dear Father, thank you for this reminder that there is nothing in us that is so bad that you will not touch us. Help us to bring the very worst part of us to you today.

BP

WEDNESDAY 2 SEPTEMBER *Luke 17:11–13 (RSV)*

At a distance

He was met by ten men suffering from a dreaded skin-disease. They stood at a distance…

At the time when the law was established regarding the treatment of lepers in Jewish society, survival of the whole tribe of Israel could have been threatened if skin disease was allowed to run unchecked. (As a teenager I saw the effect of unchecked disease in Morocco where every other beggar had pus-weeping sores). It would have decimated the community. However, the solution put forward was exceptionally harsh: 'The leper who has the disease shall wear torn clothes and let the hair of his head hang loose, and he shall cover his upper lip and cry, "Unclean, unclean." …he shall dwell alone in a habitation outside the camp." (Leviticus 13:45–46)

This example of both verbal and non-verbal communication had not changed one iota between the times of Moses and Jesus. Fear had turned these poor sufferers into non-people. Sometimes we're not really aware of how lacking in compassion we've become until brought face to face with our prejudice.

We are involved with an organization which is trying to build long-term care homes for the profoundly disabled. Its founders have a totally dependent grown-up daughter, and it was their fear of what would happen to her after their death that led them to devote vast amounts of their time, money and energy to this project. Imagine their disbelief and hurt when, after finally getting land and planning permission, they have found themselves met by a wall of hatred from the village where they plan to build their home.

Profound disability is not contagious. The villagers just don't want to see it. Surely that couldn't ever be us? Or could it? Can we honestly say that we have never ever, where two or three of us have gathered together, created a leper? Someone who is to be kept out of what we are planning, however subtly, because of something which they cannot control or they are unaware of— their size, their colour, their age, their tendency to do or say something which we have agreed we don't approve of?

Father, forgive us, for we have become complacent about what we do.

BP

THURSDAY 3 SEPTEMBER Luke 6:27–36 (GNB)

Be merciful

Be merciful just as your Father is merciful.

Every now and then something happens to us and, as a result, we know that we will never be the same again. Last year I watched a television programme about an autistic little boy called Jordan. It was a fly-on-the-wall documentary about a fortnight he and his parents spent at a radical organization in America which has pioneered a new treatment for autism, centred on a cosy, bright room they call 'The Playroom'.

Jordan's parents loved him dearly but had been unable to get close to this highly disturbed little fellow. His mum freely admitted that she needed to learn how to play, and much of the film concentrated on her floundering but determined efforts to do so, but it was the learning curve his father had to make that particularly moved me. In conversations with staff he revealed that he saw Jordan as a lovely child gripped by the crab-claws of autism. Such a shame, from his point of view.

Workers helped him to see how blinded he had been to the fact that Jordan's autism was an integral part of him and that if he was able to enter into his son's world and accept him as he was, amazing joys were to be found.

Princess Diana was insecure, Florence Nightingale had a terrible temper; not in themselves enviable characteristics. In fact, rather a shame they had to have them really! And yet it was Princess Diana's insecurity that fuelled her extraordinary empathy with the lost and lonely, and Florence Nightingale's fierce temper that cut through the fudge of bureaucracy in acquiring supplies for the Crimean injured.

Jordan's autism wasn't a monster to be hated, it was as much a part of him as Florence's temper, and as apparently impossible to change. What Jesus did, and what we are called to do, is to enter the world of those we fear or find difficult to love.

Dear Father, help us to recognize, as Jesus always did, the seeds of good within the hearts of those we have rejected, so that flowers will bud and bloom in the lives which until now had appeared desert wastelands.

BP

Friday 4 September *Luke 17:12–15; Luke 5:27–31 (GNB)*

Our only hope

They stood at a distance and shouted, 'Jesus! Master! Take pity on us!'

'People who are well do not need a doctor…'

The lepers were powerless to do anything to make themselves acceptable. All they could do was cry out, 'Jesus! Master! Take pity on us!' exactly as they were. Race and class had no place in their world. Samaritan and Jew, rich and poor, old and young were herded together in the ghetto. Jesus was literally their only hope.

In a world that has largely rejected its creator and redeemer, most of society has lost sight of the fact that Jesus is their only hope. It is easy to see how much *they* need him, isn't it? Easy to preach the need for healing from the disease of sin—from a safe distance, mind you, for fear of contamination.

But what of us? The truth is that Jesus is *our* only hope against the pharisaical leprosy of arrogance and hardness that keeps us outside his kingdom. While Jesus was on earth he did not mince his words when describing what he thought of the behaviour of 'whitewashed sepulchres' who claimed to represent him but who were responsible for most of the taboos and empty rituals governing the Jewish religion. We too need to cry out to him to have pity on us, but that will only happen when we have learned to acknowledge our particular disease as rampant within us, filthy and incurable.

Only when we realize that we are unable to change ourselves to make ourselves acceptable in his sight can God reach out and put his arms around all that we are, and heal us. I really find it quite awful to see myself as my beloved Saviour must see me, yet the glorious truth for me and you is that it doesn't have to be like this. Today we can be clean.

Dear Father, today hear our cry, 'Jesus! Master! Take pity on us!' and in his name please cleanse us from all unrighteousness.

BP

SATURDAY 5 SEPTEMBER *Luke 17:15–19 (GNB)*

Thank you

When one of them saw that he was healed, he came back...

They were going home! The word of Jesus meant, not only that they would no longer suffer the acute discomfort of their illness, but also that they could walk though the door of their homes, kiss their children, cuddle, hug and be touched. They could again linger, laughing and talking, over a meal, walk with dignity into the streets, jostle in the market square and even worship in the temple. Not surprising really that nine ran off to the priest without stopping to say thank you.

Interestingly, it is the one who perhaps had a little less to go back to who came to give thanks. As a leper he had been an equal with his Jewish fellow-sufferers. Now he must return to the stigma of being a Samaritan, no longer even allowed to speak to those he had been living so closely with. Maybe it was because he had grown up with an understanding of what it was like to be despised that he was so much more aware.

Some years ago we hosted a very deprived little Londoner for his summer holidays. At first our boys felt a sort of kindly benevolence towards him, introducing him to such unknown luxuries as duvet covers and bacon. He loved the latter and demanded 'them strips' at every possible occasion, but *he* clearly pitied *us* too. Amazed to discover that we put milk on our cereal, he was very scornful, urging us to try water "cos 'sbetter'. He was surprisingly aware of my needs, and after he had happily returned home (with no regrets, except perhaps for the loss of 'them strips') I thought of him often.

I found myself wishing my boys were equally aware of when I was tired or needed a cup of tea!

Dear Father, some of us don't feel much cop. Help us today to be aware of the qualities which you were only able to nurture in us because we were going through tough times, and thank you that because of you we are all going home.

BP

Sunday 6 September · Romans 6:1–3 (NIV)

Battles

Shall we go on sinning, so that grace may increase? By no means! We died to sin; how can we live in it any longer? Or don't you know that all of us who were baptized into Christ Jesus were baptized into his death?

I sometimes think that Romans should be a two-way conversation. It should be written as a dialogue rather than a letter. Paul battles his way through vital theology as if he were explaining to someone standing in front of him, arguing his point, anticipating his opponent's next objection. Here he is now, having just established that sin cannot outstrip grace (Romans 5:20), then quickly asserting that this does not license us to go wild.

My mind is a bit like Romans. It struggles away, coming from this angle and then that, no sooner getting hold of some essential truth than finding itself up against opposition from another quarter. So round it goes again. 'I'll never sin like that again!' I declare to myself. 'It feels so good to obey God, I'll stand firm in the next test.' Then whoops! So busy looking proudly upwards I don't notice the pot-hole and there I am down again.

Paul is hammering out doctrine for us in exhausting detail, and our daily experience needs the working truth it contains. We don't want to sin. We crave the grace of God. We want to know that sin has no mastery over us. We need to understand how we died to sin because Christ did, and we are baptized into him. But only the Holy Spirit can burn this into a real part of our everyday lives.

'I will give you a new heart and put a new spirit in you; I will remove from you your heart of stone and give you a heart of flesh' (Ezekiel 36:26).

Lord, I bring my fallible self to you today. Help me by your Spirit to experience with head and heart that my true self is alive to you and dead to the call of sin. Teach me. Amen.

DA

MONDAY 7 SEPTEMBER   Romans 6:4b–5 (NIV)

Certainty

Just as Christ was raised from the dead through the glory of the Father, we too may live a new life. If we have been united with him like this in his death, we will certainly also be united with him in his resurrection.

This is not a certain world. It seems we all become increasingly aware of its fragility, its uncertainty. We are bombarded by the media with news of the latest tragedy, from the small to the epic. There are days when I have to brace myself to hear the latest. The only constant is change.

So no wonder some of us struggle to appreciate fully the security of our faith. Nothing else around us ever stays the same. But these words of Paul are precisely what we need in order to keep our balance. If only we can see past the cares and trials that so easily preoccupy us, these verses can bring us such a glorious breath of fresh air. For here is a double promise. Not only a future to look forward to, wrapped up securely in the unstoppable power of Jesus' resurrection, one day to be released into the freedom of heaven, being with him. But also a new life here and now.

Life without Christ has gone. It died when he did. The new has already begun. Of course, we know that. But in the humdrum of daily routines, responsibilities and stress we can lose sight of its potential. In an uncertain world, we can have certainty. More than that—we *do* have certainty. It is a fact. No matter how far life may fall to pieces around us, it is still sure. If we allow its security to grip us at gut level, then we can face the challenges and changes of day-to-day life with a cast-iron spiritual constitution.

We have access to the most awesome truths the world could ever know. Christ died for you. You have new life. Resurrection power lives in you today. Use it.

Try 1 John 4:13–16.

DA

TUESDAY 8 SEPTEMBER　　　　　　　　　　Romans 6:11 (NIV)
Choice

Count yourselves dead to sin but alive to God in Christ Jesus.

Another day. What do you face? Are there dependent toddlers demanding your attention? Or is the challenge to whizz through the list before leaving the house in time for work? Perhaps you face sickness in yourself or a loved one. Or pain in your most important relationships. Perhaps it's just one of those days which looks like a mountain impossible to scale.

So often it feels as if life gives us very little choice. There are so many things which just have to be done. As Steve Martin said in the film *Parenthood*, 'All my life is "have-to".' There are so many demands to be met just to keep life going, let alone coping with crises, that all our energies go into stopping the nutcracker from finishing us off.

Doesn't sound much like being alive to God, does it? Or being 'in' Christ Jesus—knowing the dynamic experience of living with someone who has defeated sin, burst through death, speaks resurrection into lifelessness and is the ultimate resolution of all things?

How do we span the gap between our often struggling existence and Paul's assertion that we are alive to God? I wonder if the key is in those first two words, 'Count yourselves…'. Paul says that we do have a choice. We have more choice than we think. He urges us to reckon ourselves, to make a decision. We *are* out of the clutches of the old ways of living. We *are* alive to God. The transaction has been completed. We are not powerless. The truth is that we can choose to appropriate the potential of our lives. It may seem like an impossible decision to make, when circumstances and internal strife threaten to overwhelm us. But somewhere in the maelstrom of thoughts and emotions the door of choice is there.

Can we take a deep breath and choose to plant our mustard seed of faith, and believe that it will grow?

If choices seem non-existent, ask God to show you where they are.

DA

WEDNESDAY 9 SEPTEMBER *Romans 6:13 (NIV)*

Choosing righteousness

Do not offer the parts of your body to sin, as instruments of wickedness, but rather offer yourselves to God, as those who have been brought from death to life; and offer the parts of your body to him as instruments of righteousness,

It really is up to us. Perhaps today would be a good day to wrest some space for yourself in a punishing schedule and consider your choices. Why not decide to keep some quality time for yourself, however brief, and use it to test the truth of Romans 6?

If we truly are 'in Christ' (Romans 6:11), if our lives are 'hidden with Christ in God' (Colossians 3:3), then the basis for our lives is sound and the potential limitless. If the cross of Christ which achieved all this for us is the beginning of everything, then our starting point can also be in God rather than in situations, personality or problems. So whatever we face, we face it with Christ, and with choice.

When it comes to offering 'the parts of [our] body to sin', we can face a plethora of choices. I find myself conjuring up everything from adultery to gossip—and too much chocolate cake. The trouble is that some wickedness does feel fun. Why do I respond more readily to the instant gratification of calorie-laden goo, than to the everlasting benefits of the best friendship I'll ever have? It is ridiculous when I think about it—when I remember that I do have a choice. I also suspect that God cares less about my addiction to cocoa than he does about other wrong choices I make. Perhaps tying myself in knots about cream cakes is a good distraction from acknowledging the areas where I never think about choosing the way of life instead of death. Which brings us back to anything from adultery to gossip.

Don't risk it. Consider your choices. Be alive to God.

Dear Lord, help!

DA

THURSDAY 10 SEPTEMBER · Romans 6:14–15 (NIV)

Grace

For sin shall not be your master, because you are not under law, but under grace. What then? Shall we sin because we are not under law but under grace? By no means!

For many of us, becoming a Christian was like turning on the colours in a black-and-white world. To discover that there really was Someone out there, and that that Someone loved us personally, was similar to moving from an ice-bound country to a strange but beautiful land of warmth. Everything looked different. But as we explore our new world, sometimes we react to it as if it were the old one. We can't quite believe that it is different. It's as if we close our eyes in disbelief that it could be this good, and then can only see the old world on the inside of our eyelids. After all, we knew it so well.

Is this part of the reason why Paul talks us through the truth with such dedication and persuasion? He seems desperate for his readers to comprehend fully what has happened to them. He wants us to enjoy our new-found country to the utmost. Not any more the exhausting round of trying to live according to a set of rules to get right with God. Or to get right with each other, or even with ourselves. That's not what life in God's country is about. Here we live in a consistent atmosphere of grace—undeserved mercy. Here we are free to look back and remember how the laws in the old land served only to condemn and never to enable. Here we can luxuriate in free-given forgiveness. Jesus really has done it all. 'It is for freedom that Christ has set us free' (Galatians 5:1). Here we are at liberty to choose life and a new beginning every morning.

Do we dare to open our eyes fully, stretch out our limbs and glory in the freedom we have?

Read Jeremiah 31:33. Are you enjoying being under grace? If not, talk to God about it today.

DA

FRIDAY 11 SEPTEMBER — Romans 6:21 (NIV)

Reality

What benefit did you reap at that time from the things you are now ashamed of? Those things result in death!

This is real 'wake up and smell the coffee' sentiment from Paul. Just in case we haven't got the message yet in all he has written, here he steps up close, takes hold of our shoulders and gives us a good shake. Don't you see, he says, all the things you used to do, everything you lived for before you decided for Christ, it was all to no avail. It wasn't going anywhere. There was no eternal perspective to bring the day-to-day to life. Indeed, some of what you were involved in brings you shame to think about now. Don't you realize there was no point to it, no benefit at all?

Some of us can easily see and disown the old ways. Others of us find the issues are not so clear-cut. But all of us face times when the call of the old world gets a bit strong. We are not quite sure whether the benefits of the old really are that empty. Perhaps slavery to sin and law wasn't so bad after all. What are the voices that tempt you to renege on your choice for real life? Is it compromising with materialism and looking for life in the hypermarket? Not that shopping is wrong in itself, but you won't find eternity there. Or perhaps you hear the cry of the 'if only's—if only I had that job, a bigger family, more friends, loads of money. If only I was different. If only life was different. Again, not that aspirations are out, but even achieving them brings limited satisfaction. Or perhaps temptation is disguising itself as happiness, and you can't believe it would really be wrong. What is it for you?

Listen to Paul. He does not mince his words. We're talking eternity here. Let's not get side-tracked by things which bring no benefit.

Jesus said, 'I am the way and the truth and the life' (John 14:6). Think about it.

DA

SATURDAY 12 SEPTEMBER *Romans 6:23 (NIV)*

The gift

For the wages of sin is death, but the gift of God is eternal life in Christ Jesus our Lord.

I seem to have heard the first half of this verse quoted far more often than the whole thing. And in the days when the business of life, God and the meaning of the universe was distinctly overwhelming and frightening, 'the wages of sin is death' would send a *frisson* of fear down my spine. I could not see how I could ever be free of its condemning power. I knew only too well that I could never live up to all that God expected of me and these words served only to enhance my terror. It all seemed so difficult and dread-full. I knew sin had a price tag and that usually payment began in the here and now, a little dying before death. I'd hurt people and seen the results. I'd lied, and suffered for it. I'd stolen, and ruined my conscience for years. The wages of sin is death.

Then one day I heard the rest of the verse. There is a very big 'but' there. It was actually hard to listen to, because I had got pretty efficient at self-condemnation and probably over-paying for my guilt. But the 'but' gradually broke through. God has given me—given us—a gift. Unlike sin's wages, it is not earned or initiated by us. God has paid the price so that we can enjoy the freedom of life under grace. Life without condemnation. Life eternal. Real life, fresh air, warmth and colour. The freedom to make choices. The unbelievable companionship of God himself.

We may still be on the edge of exploring all that the gift of eternal life means, but we can learn that when God says it is real, then it is real. There can't be a better way than God's, can there?

Read John 6:35–40. Father, help me to fully appreciate your free gift. Jesus, thank you for giving me life. Holy Spirit, fill me with the truth. Amen.

DA

SUNDAY 13 SEPTEMBER — Romans 8:1–4 (RSV)

Freedom

There is therefore now no condemnation for those who are in Christ Jesus.

In writing the book of Romans, Paul was eager to convince not only Gentiles but also Jews that he was legitimately a missionary to all. But he begins chapter 8 by emphasizing that the Christian struggle is about sin, and not lack of Judaic credentials or status or obedience to the Law, and he highlights our only claim for justification—Jesus.

The huge crowd from earth stood before the throne of the living God and angels filled the air with their singing. The Christian shivered as she heard her name called. She was next.

She had tried to do her very best on earth. Never deliberately hurting a living soul, not once. But suddenly she wasn't thinking of the number of times she'd been to church or the catechism she knew, or the commandments she could recite backwards, or the charity boxes she'd filled or the help she'd given to her friends.

The eyes that now met hers were full of such love and purity and goodness that her whole being was overwhelmed with light and she saw the dark depths of her soul—her lack of love and her own self-love.

The great Creator's voice thundered, 'Who judges this woman?' Then she heard the voice of the being of light in front of her. The one whose eyes were pure love. 'I do,' he said.

'The price for this person's sin is death,' proclaimed the thundering voice. 'Who is to pay?'

'I have paid,' said the being of light, and in that moment this same Jesus took her small, trembling self into his arms and hugged until her tears of sorrow turned to tears of joy.

Lord, help me to live as a free human being. Free from fear and past sin. I want to live your love. I know I'll fail. God, forgive me. Thank you that your success, your victory over sin and death, is my passport to freedom of spirit and that hug. Please, I need that justification so badly. Amen.

HMcD

MONDAY 14 SEPTEMBER   *Romans 8:5–11 (RSV)*

Two paths

For those who live according to the flesh set their minds on the things of the flesh, but those who live according to the Spirit set their minds on the things of the Spirit.

She walked to the crossroads twenty times or more that day before she realized it wasn't one crossroads but a million. The road divided into two paths each moment of her existence. Every thought was a choice to think evil or think good. To see that person in the negative or the positive. To speak harsh words or words of peace, to criticize or encourage, to stay silent or challenge another's bad jokes or evil intent to a third person. She could satisfy the body or feed the soul. Those two roads led into many forests and if she was to choose the road less travelled then she would have to desire Jesus more than all other needs on earth.

But how could his gentle, loving voice of mercy be heard above the deafening roar of her timetable, the daily demands of routine and sustenance and shelter and clothing and family and work and hormones and mortgage and cousin Maud's inopportune visits and the telephone and the constant demands of you-know-who? STOP! She took control and stilled her racing mind with the Saviour's promises until he became her only focus and her single intent.

Jesus, I'm going to believe that your Spirit works in me. Believe it when my body screams for attention. When the media threaten to depreciate my value by the alternative images of life and living they present. When temptation bites and dazzles. When I'm exhausted by my own efforts. When my immediate physical and material surroundings dominate so much that they almost convince me that there is nothing more to life than them. I'm going to believe that you are in me, for you promised and you are faithful. I set my mind this day, not on the flesh, but on you. Guard and guide my feet along that road less travelled. I belong to you. Amen.
HMcD

TUESDAY 15 SEPTEMBER   *Romans 8:12–17 (RSV)*

Inheritance

For you did not receive the spirit of slavery to fall back into fear, but you have received the spirit of sonship.

Paul wrote this within a culture where slavery was normal. A slave could be killed at a moment's notice if his master took the whim. Fear bears real teeth in that situation.

She waged war on the enemy. It was 'death to the body' at every turn. She spiritually pummelled it, exercised it, denied it, handcuffed it, shackled its freedom and basically put it in irons. All in a valiant attempt to subdue it to the will of Christ. Yet Satan managed to end the day on a sour note by reminding her that she had still failed to be perfect and sinless.

If you want to empty a bucket of its contents of silt-ridden water and you are unable to turn it upside-down, then the only way to cleanse it is to fill the bucket with a substance that is heavier and more solid than the muddy water. Let Christ fill every part of us with himself who is 'the rock', and watch the mud and silt spill out over the rim.

Fear flees then for a son, a daughter, of the living God. Paul uses 'Abba', the intimate word akin to 'Daddy', the word the Lord used from the cross to his Father in heaven. Sin makes slaves; God's love produces sons and daughters. In Roman law adoption merely brought an orphan under the authority of the new father, but Paul understood the process in the context of conferring upon the child the rights and status of an heir. This is the amazing truth which Paul is communicating to his readers. Jesus, God's Son, shares his inheritance with us whether we deserve it or not, and which of us does?

Abba Father, how shall I love you?
  Child, let me give you heaven.
Abba Father, how shall I purge sin from my life?
  Child, my Spirit wants to speak with you.
Abba, I want to be a better person.
  Child, let me be a closer God.
Daddy, what is this that cries from the depths of me?
  Child, it is I.

HMcD

WEDNESDAY 16 SEPTEMBER　　　　　　　*Romans 8:18–25 (RSV)*

The big picture

I consider that the sufferings of this present time are not worth comparing with the glory that is to be revealed to us.

When I was young I used to work on a great many jigsaw puzzles. I would study piece by piece for hours trying to discover where they fitted into the big picture. The ones which took the most time to complete, sometimes even days, were those where the lid of the box had been lost and no 'big picture' was available to provide clues for the finished pattern.

It was good practice for life, where no finished picture is to be seen while we work on our lives. That is why pain feels so burdensome, emotional wounds cut so deeply, failure produces such devastating disappointment. We imagine that what we see is all there is. But God knows better.

Paul had an inkling of this in his own life with the 'thorn in the flesh' that he could not remove, and he shares the insight with us. The pain we feel is not just ours. We are part of the continuing struggle of the entire universe as it bears the 'labour pains' of new birth. The death and resurrection of Jesus is for the remaking, not just of humankind, but of all creation, the environment, the entire kingdom of earth as it seeks to aspire towards the kingdom of heaven. Decay, disease, disaster, sin and death are all part of the old world kingdom. In Jesus we are sons and daughters of his kingdom and the big picture will show us the finished product.

Lord, I long to be your witness in the world. Help me live in such a manner that my very surroundings may know the renewal of God's touch through me.

But, dear Father, this birthing is hard. Never did I imagine these thrusting, tearing, searing labour pains. No one prepared me for this, Lord.

Child, see the empty tomb. Welcome to my victory.
See, my child, you have life. My labour pains gave birth to you.

HMcD

THURSDAY 17 SEPTEMBER   Romans 8:26–28 (RSV)

Trusting

We know that in everything God works for good with those who love him, who are called according to his purpose.

Often we spend a great deal of time outlining to God what is best for the world. Telling him how things are and how they should work and how we feel. As if he doesn't know already!

A glance at the psalms always reminds me that it's when we are in the depths of despair that our conversation with God becomes most real. (For examples, see Psalm 22 or Psalm 69.) Pain cannot be 'dressed up' in pious platitudes or quaint traditional phrases. When a person is hurting all they feel is the hurt. 'Help!' says it all when things are so bad that there is nothing left to be said. There is no greater tutor of prayer than pain, whether physical or emotional. It stings our agendas to a silent halt and enables us to open our hearts and lives to the mastery of God's Spirit. But are our inarticulate stabs at communication with an almighty God who is in control all we have to rely upon? Paul highlights grounds for hope.

The Holy Spirit knows how to pray, even when we do not. Maybe we should spend less time wrestling with words and more listening to him as the Spirit quietly and powerfully brings to the Saviour everything we would have said if only we had known how, 'with groanings that cannot be uttered'. Trust is being still and believing that God's agenda is moving towards the very best for us regardless of the external evidence of our present circumstances. He will not refuse to enter into them with us because he has plans for us; plans designed with one single motivation—unconditional love. Even a standing still in trust is a moving forward in his will.

Father, I don't know what to say.
Listen, my child.
Dear God, this pain is too much.
I know.
Jesus, how can I fix it?
Trust me.
Lord, I need to know what to do.
Do you?

HMcD

FRIDAY 18 SEPTEMBER   Romans 8:29–34 (RSV)

The 'boss'

What then shall we say to this? If God is for us, who is against us?

When the apostle was on the road to Damascus, that blinding light of Christ's presence which left him without physical sight for three days gave him the precious and painful gift of time to reflect.

Reflection on his past life: the lofty prestige, zealous religious observance, intellectual knowledge and Roman citizenship—all led to that road to Damascus. Even while Paul's free-will persecuted the Christians, God was working to ensure that he was the official present at Stephen's stoning (Acts 7:58). It was Paul who held the coats of the stone-throwers and, as a result, heard one of the best speeches of witness to Christ recorded in the New Testament. Paul learnt that seemingly chance happenings were often part of a thread running through his life that brought him in surrender to the resurrected Christ. God does not force but he does not waste either. He wasted no experience of Paul's life and he will waste nothing of ours.

He is ultimately in control. It does not mean we have no freedom of choice. He calls, we can say 'no'. He loves, we can choose to hate. He bestows blessings, we can reject the offer of such gifts. But he's 'the boss' and he chose us even before we were aware of our need of him.

The Christian life is a partnership with a living God. Not an equal partnership—he is God, after all—but a partnership nevertheless. We are neither robots nor clones, but God wills that we should be brothers and sisters whose lives become modelled upon the example of Jesus.

Today are you feeling surrounded by negative and unjust criticism? Remember, our defence against all attack and our own sense of failure and unworthiness is God himself—that's some defence!

Father, forgive me for my fears. You have destined my time and purpose upon the earth and I need no justification more than that. Thank you for trusting me, Lord, enough to give me life. Amen.

HMcD

SATURDAY 19 SEPTEMBER   Romans 8:35–39 (RSV)
Strength in him

In all these things we are more than conquerors through him who loved us.

Another human foible Paul and I share is that we make lists. Well, maybe it's not a bad trait after all. Without lists how could our memories possibly cope? Shopping lists, chore lists, Christmas card lists, prayer lists, 'things to be attempted when I can get round to it' lists. The trouble is, one woman's inclusive list might exclude the very thing which is top of the next girl's memo pad.

Mind you, this list of Paul's is pretty comprehensive. It includes just about every power and fear and threat and terror imaginable to his contemporary world. (Verse 36 echoes Psalm 44:22. This is the stuff of martyrs.)

What about our struggle? It would be good to go slowly through Paul's list and identify the parallels in our lives. Name our daily tribulation and distress. Face our areas of persecution. Recognize in what respects we are hungry or naked or in peril. What are the dark powers with whom we wrestle in this twentieth century, and are we determined to conquer our past and present and vanquish fears for things to come?

'Nor height, nor depth, nor any other creature, can separate us from the love of God which is in Christ Jesus our Lord.' Do we know that we can trust him with the full height of our fears, with the depths of our agony, with every monster that attempts to stalk our daily living? For God is greater and stronger and closer than everything on our list. Hanging from a precipice? Feel the cords of his strong love about you. You can rely on it!

Jesus, I know that the spiritual forces of darkness are as real today as they were in Paul's time, they just manifest themselves in more sophisticated ways. Clear my sight to recognize my attackers. When I feel separated from you help me to remember that you do not change. Thank you for never erecting barriers. Thank you for being here, for me, always. Amen.
HMcD

Sunday 20 September   Psalm 102:6–7 (NRSV)
Solitude

I am like an owl of the wilderness, like a little owl of the waste places. I lie awake; I am like a lonely bird on the housetop.

The next two weeks are going to be spent looking at solitude and silence and how, as women, we can use aspects of these disciplines to deepen our relationship with Jesus. To start with, I want to take a quick look at what I do *not* mean by 'solitude'.

I expect if you asked someone what they thought solitude is, they would answer, 'Being alone.' Being alone in itself is not solitude, in the sense that we will be studying, and you don't need to be alone to enter into this solitude either. The bird alone on the roof in today's verse is not experiencing solitude, but loneliness and isolation. Loneliness and isolation are the result of a lack of communication between ourselves and God, or our spouse, our family members and our church fellowship. This lack of communication can produce a great sense of affliction in the life of the lonely person, which is not good for the spiritual health.

We know from the creation story in Genesis that it is not good for man (or woman!) to be alone, and often the only way to combat that loneliness is to restore the lines of communication, first with God, and second with our fellow human beings. This may involve a great deal of humility in that we may need to ask forgiveness from God and those we have offended. It may mean a great deal of self-sacrifice in learning to put the interests of others before our own so that fellowship can again begin to flourish.

Before we go further and look at 'solitude', take stock of your life. Are the communication lines clear and functioning between you and the Lord, between you and your family or workmates? Solitude is an attitude of inner peace. If there is unforgiveness and strife in our life, solitude can be impossible to find. Ask God's help to start putting things right.

AS

MONDAY 21 SEPTEMBER *Isaiah 30:15; Psalm 62:5–8 (NIV)*

Repentance and rest

In repentance and rest is your salvation, in quietness and trust is your strength, but you would have none of it.

Samel Pepys, the famous English diarist, wrote, 'My wife is troubled by her lonely life.' When my children were younger and I was stuck at home with no adult company, I too was very troubled by my lonely life. That loneliness, compounded by post-natal depression and the sheer exhaustion of having three babies in two and a half years, caused a very bitter root to spring up in my life. I was no good on my own and I certainly was not pleasant in company.

My personal journey towards finding solitude to replace loneliness and silence in the midst of domestic chaos started with repentance and rest, and led on into quietness and trust. I had to confess my bitterness, rage and anger towards God, my family and the church and ask for forgiveness in return. Only then was I able to experience that inner rest that allowed me to stop finding any excuse to avoid being still in God's presence. Until then I was frightened that if I was still before God for too long, he would point out all the things I was trying to batten down and hide!

After this life-changing experience, I had about a year of quietness of heart and learning to trust. The children still prevented me from going out and domestic life was still noisy and busy, but I was not afraid of being alone any more and happy to stay at home with the Lord as my 'adult company'. It was time to learn not to fuss unduly, but trust God for his wisdom, strength and insight into the situations I had to cope with.

Meditate on the following scripture and turn it into prayer:
'But me she forgot,' declares the Lord. 'Therefore I am now going to allure her; I will lead her into the desert and speak tenderly to her. There I will give her back her vineyards, and will make the Valley of Achor [trouble, anguish, crying] a door of hope. There she will sing as in the days of her youth.' (Hosea 2:13b–15a, NIV)

AS

TUESDAY 22 SEPTEMBER   Psalm 27:4–5 (NRSV)

God—our 'sole-attitude'

One thing I asked of the Lord, that will I seek after: to live in the house of the Lord all the days of my life, to behold the beauty of the Lord, and to inquire in his temple. For he will hide me in his shelter in the day of trouble; he will conceal me under the cover of his tent.

I have struggled for quite a while to decide how I can describe or define 'solitude'. I have talked about how solitude is not being alone in the sense of being lonely, but solitude does need times of being alone if it is to be cultivated. I think Richard Foster was given great insight to call solitude 'the portable sanctuary of the heart'. It is that 'inner attentiveness' to Jesus that we carry with us through the day that is God's gift of grace to us when we discipline ourselves to practise living constantly in his presence.

Solitude is about being in a right relationship with God; about resting in him; it is the call to 'abide' that Jesus makes to his disciples; it is the 'knowing' of God in the depths of our being that itself is the work of the Holy Spirit. Solitude is the relinquishing of our own will in favour of God's will, the hearing of the 'still small voice' and the innate desire to obey without question. Solitude is the ability of the heart and mind to be so lost in love for the Saviour that it desires only to gaze and gaze upon him.

I will be quite honest and say that my experience of true solitude as I understand it and have described it has been none too frequent. But those few glimpses God has granted to me when I have had even the shortest amount of time and space to open myself to him have been more than enough to sustain me through 'the day of trouble', when I have had to take my 'portable sanctuary' out into the world again.

'My soul longs, indeed it faints for the courts of the Lord; my heart and my flesh sing for joy to the living God' (Psalm 84:2, NRSV).

AS

WEDNESDAY 23 SEPTEMBER *Revelation 4 (NRSV)*

Come up here

After this I looked, and there in heaven a door stood open! And the first voice, which I had heard speaking to me like a trumpet, said, 'Come up here...'

In the temple in Jerusalem during biblical times, the innermost sanctuary was the 'Holiest Place'. It was seen as the earthly counterpart of God's throne in heaven. Only the priests were allowed to enter here, and then only once a year, on the Day of Atonement. Such was the privilege of being allowed to enter 'God's earthly presence' that the priests used to draw lots to see who would go in.

Of course there is no physical temple today for us to desire to enter, but the New Testament tells us that we ourselves are the temple of God's Holy Spirit. In the inner silence of our hearts we can enter the holiest place of God's presence and can enjoy in solitude the most beautiful of spiritual disciplines: beholding God's heavenly throne in devotional prayer.

If our inner attentiveness is to be fixed on the sovereignty of God, what we can do is to meditate on the throne of God as described in Revelation 4. Read the passage slowly, use all your senses to enter the scene: see the colours, bask in the light, hear the sounds, smell the incense—the prayers of the saints—enter the worship. Allow this meditation to let you respond in silent or vocal worship.

If this is repeated over a course of weeks, gradually the passage is burned on our memory and we move from meditation to contemplation, which is pure, unaided adoration. If we are really blessed, contemplation may turn occasionally to vision and we enter an atmosphere thick with angels.

'How awesome is this place! This is none other than the house of God, and this is the gate of heaven' (Genesis 28:17, NRSV).

AS

THURSDAY 24 SEPTEMBER   1 Kings 19:1–13 (NRSV)

After the fire

He said, 'Go out and stand on the mountain before the Lord, for the Lord is about to pass by.' Now there was a great wind, so strong that it was splitting mountains ... but the Lord was not in the wind; and after the wind an earthquake, but the Lord was not in the earthquake; and after the earthquake a fire, but the Lord was not in the fire, and after the fire a sound of sheer silence. When Elijah heard it, he wrapped his face in his mantle and went out and stood at the entrance of the cave.

On the few occasions that I have managed to get a baby-sitter who is willing to miss a Sunday evening service to let me go instead, at the end of the worship time I have found myself with the same vision in my mind, quite unprompted. There was God's holy mountain glowing in earthy colours of bronze and gold. Rising from behind the mountain and gathering over the summit has been a billowing grey-black cloud and I have felt the Spirit saying, 'The Lord is on his holy mountain, stand in awe at what he will do.'

I would never go so far as to say that I knew what God was about to do, but it seems to me that after quite a few 'partying years' in the British church, it may be time to start to reawaken in ourselves the knowledge that our God is an awesome God and that he reigns in power, and we can do nothing other than stand in awe-filled silence before him.

We have spent two days looking at worship and silence in the throne-room of heaven. The power and glory of God that we have glimpsed in that place can also be seen in part on earth, his footstool.

Dwelling on the greatness and power of God brings us to an abrupt, silent halt. Like Elijah, all we can do is shield our eyes from his holiness, come into his presence and wait for what he whispers to our soul.

'Holy, holy, holy is the Lord of hosts; the whole earth is full of his glory' (Isaiah 6:3, NRSV).

AS

FRIDAY 25 SEPTEMBER Psalm 90:1–12 (NRSV)

The sacrament of the moment

For a thousand years in your sight are like yesterday when it is past, or like a watch in the night… So teach us to count our days that we may gain a wise heart.

Life today is not just crowded with people and noise, it is also very rushed and stressed. All day long we say things like, 'Hurry up, you'll be late for school', 'We'll take the car, there's no time to walk', and so it goes on. Before we know it the day has rushed by and we are left in an exhausted heap, wondering quite what we have accomplished.

Slowing down the pace of our lives can help predispose our inner selves to solitude and silence. Rather than racing thoughtlessly from one task to the next, worrying about how to fit everything into the day, it is much more beneficial to realize that 'what happens to us at each moment by God's order is precisely what for us is the holiest, the best, the most divine thing that can happen' (J.P. Caussade, SJ). So why not slow down or stop and enjoy that moment and seek to hear God speaking through the task in hand, because 'the more we apply ourselves to our little task … the more God diversifies and beautifies it. On the background of simple love and obedience, his hands love to trace the most beautiful details' (J.P. Caussade, SJ).

I was struggling through the bedtime routine the other night, determined to get to my typing. It was hopeless, the baby would not settle. In the end I abandoned myself to the Lord's will for that moment and enjoyed a time of quiet, lying next to Sam and stroking his hair as he drifted into sleep, and listened to God's Spirit whispering to my heart as to how the Father similarly cradles us in his arms and gives us comfort and rest.

Lord, help me to slow down today and constantly ask, 'What do you want me to do?' Help me to hear your voice through every action, however lowly. Amen.

AS

SATURDAY 26 SEPTEMBER *Ecclesiastes 3:1–14 (NRSV)*

Equanimity

For everything there is a season, and a time for every matter under heaven.

'Equa-what?' Equanimity basically means 'having an equal mind', 'learning to hold all things in balance', or knowing that there is 'a season for every activity under heaven' and trying to put that into practice. Why should this matter so much in relation to perfecting solitude and inner silence?

If an individual or a family can establish a firm (but flexible!) daily, weekly and monthly routine that adjusts with the seasons and provides a time for all that is necessary, the stress and strain factors on the people involved can be significantly reduced. This is particularly effective if passive and active tasks are carefully interspersed and time made for personal space. Against this background of stability it is much easier to cultivate inner silence and solitude than against a raging sea of ever-fluctuating chaos.

How do I know this? Because I have tried it. When the family and I know what is going on and what is likely to happen, then peace reigns in our house, even if it is the 'noisy peace' of happily playing children. Then I am more likely to be able to make my 'sole-attitude' one that is attentive towards Jesus, than when the storm waters are raging around me. For example, although it may sound quite old-fashioned, our children all have an hour quietly in their rooms after lunch at the weekends. This helps balance the activity of the morning and helps them calm down and learn to be happy with their own company, and eventually with the Lord's. It also gives exhausted parents time to gather breath for the next sprint!

Take a look at your routine. What needs to be balanced, cut short or cut out? Warning: make changes slowly with your spouse's approval!

Drop thy still dews of quietness,
Till all our strivings cease;
Take from our souls the strain and stress,
And let our ordered lives confess
The beauty of thy peace.

J.G. WHITTIER (1807–92)

AS

SUNDAY 27 SEPTEMBER Matthew 12:36 (NRSV)

Meaningful conversation

I tell you, on the day of judgment you will have to give an account for every careless word you utter.

Thomas à Kempis wrote, 'Often I wished I had remained silent and had not been among men. But why is it that we are so ready to chatter and gossip with each other, when we so seldom return to silence without some injury to our conscience? We think to find consolation in this manner ... but this outward consolation is no small obstacle to inner and divine consolation' (*The Imitation of Christ*).

It can be very difficult to be quiet in public. As a vicar's wife, I often have to make conversation with people I don't know terribly well, and to cover my awkwardness and shyness, I ramble on about all sorts of incidents which it is not really necessary to mention. Then I come home and feel quite foolish.

We spend a lot of time in chatter because we are constantly trying to make sure that people don't misunderstand us. We may offer information because we are constantly trying to adjust other people's perceptions of us. We want to be liked and accepted or we may want to manipulate and control a person or situation. And we do all this because of our hidden insecurities and fears.

If we are trying to be attentive in our hearts and minds towards Jesus, i.e. if he is becoming our 'sole-attitude', then being quiet in public should become easier with time, as our confidence is in the Lord. We are at peace with ourselves and him and we don't need to worry about what others are thinking of us. We are no longer constantly trying to reassure ourselves by offering and fishing for comments.

It can be difficult to relinquish control to Jesus and risk being misunderstood by becoming a person of few words in public. But when I think of having to account for all the careless ones, I think it is worth a try.

When words are many, transgression is not lacking, but the prudent are restrained in speech (Proverbs 10:19, NRSV).

AS

MONDAY 28 SEPTEMBER *Proverbs 17:1; 21:9; 14:1 (NRSV)*

A quiet house

Better is a dry morsel with quiet than a house full of feasting with strife ... It is better to live in a corner of the housetop than in a house shared with a contentious wife ... The wise woman builds her house, but the foolish tears it down with her own hands.

One thing that is conducive to producing inner silence is outer silence. Children can be very noisy, but adults can be just as bad. I remember apologizing to some neighbours about the amount of noise the children made in the garden. 'Don't worry,' they replied, 'all we ever hear is you!' I was horrified!

Joking aside, this sort of noise, or let's call it what it is—incessant nagging and over-loud disciplining—is not constructive. It is foolish behaviour that 'tears down your own house' and could drive your husband to live on a corner of the roof (!) or, at the worst, stay as long as possible at work or in the study. It also exasperates and embitters children, and eventually you hear the same attitudes in their conversations with each other.

I often catch myself saying to the children' 'If you can't say anything nice, don't say anything at all!' How I could do with taking my own advice.

What makes us nag? What makes me nag? I usually get going when I am stressed because there is too much to fit into the time available and the balancing act has gone wrong. One example of this is when I take on too many writing commitments because I want us to be able to live on more than 'a dry crust' and to be able to feast a bit. But look at the cost! The first of today's verses tells us that peace and quiet is much more valuable, and really we should be happy to be able to set that before the family even if tea turns out to be beans on toast by the end of the month!

'Teach me, and I will be silent; make me understand how I have gone wrong. How forceful are honest words!' (Job 6:24–25, NRSV)

AS

TUESDAY 29 SEPTEMBER   *Revelation 8:1–5 (NRSV)*

Silence in heaven

There was silence in heaven for about half an hour.

The last couple of days have been spent looking at tempering the kind of noise we make and reducing it as necessary, at home and in the community. However, temperance of speech is not silence.

'The discipline of silence is the voluntary and temporary abstention from speaking, so that certain spiritual goals might be sought (e.g. to pray, write, study). Though there is no outward speaking there are internal dialogues with self and with God. Other times silence is maintained inwardly, also, so that God's voice might be heard more clearly' (*Spiritual Disciples of Christian Life*, Donald Whitney).

It is fair to say that silence is not generally a twentieth-century experience. In the so-called silence of my kitchen as I type late at night, I can hear cars, the central heating, clocks and domestic appliances—at least four. During the day I have the added clamour of children's videos roaring, computer games beeping, phone and doorbell ringing.

However, there are snatches of silence that occur during the day, minute retreats when we can commit ourselves to communing with God in our hearts. For me these may be walking back from school having dropped off the children, driving to the supermarket, waiting in the check-out queue (if Sam is in a good mood!), standing at the sink or in the laundry-room, etc.

Until recently I was convinced that these little oases were enough, but as I experience more of the spiritual growth that comes from solitude and silence, I realize that we have to make the effort to spend time in silence, alone, while not engaged in another activity, so we can focus our attention properly. I am sure that when there was silence in heaven for half an hour, the angels weren't busily dashing around, but silent and still, with their gaze fixed on the throne and the lamb of God.

Make an effort to sit quietly still for half an hour today and wait on the Lord. To concentrate the mind, imagine the half-hour silence in heaven.
AS

WEDNESDAY 30 SEPTEMBER   Mark 1:35 (NIV)

A solitary place

Very early in the morning, while it was still dark, Jesus got up, left the house and went off to a solitary place, where he prayed.

The best reason for making time to be alone with the Father is because Jesus gave us that example to follow.

Many mothers feel so guilty that they are unable to keep up the 'regular morning quiet time' that they give up totally, bound up by law. I have to admit that I have been in the same camp, because young children are so omnipresent, and the female conscience so ready with self-criticism. However, having tried to find a spirituality to fit my busy lifestyle as a mother, I find it amusing that I have come full circle. This time, though, it has got to be grace, and flexible grace at that!

My husband gets his hour alone in the bathroom each morning. I am surprised he hasn't dissolved by now! A regular slot would not work with my other demands, but it could be possible to work out a plan of various alternatives depending on the structure of the day.

On the days when Mark is out in the evening, I could find time once the children were in bed if I decided not to be distracted by the accounts, ironing or the sewing machine. On days when Mark is out for lunch, I could get some time during Sam's nap, if I plan not to make anything too fancy for tea. On supermarket days when Sam falls asleep on the return trip, I could sit in the car on the drive for half an hour and unpack later (with a toddler's help!) Where there is a will, there is a way.

Retire from the world each day to some private spot. Stay in the secret place till the surrounding noises begin to fade out of your heart and a sense of God's presence envelops you … Listen for the inward voice until you learn to recognize it … Gaze on Christ with the eyes of your soul. All the above is contingent on a right relation to God in Christ and daily meditation on the scriptures.
A.W. TOZER

AS

THURSDAY 1 OCTOBER　　　　　　　　Matthew 26:36–45 (NIV)

The prayer of quiet

Then Jesus went with his disciples to a place called Gethsemane, and he said to them, 'Sit here while I go over there and pray.' He took Peter and the two sons of Zebedee along with him, and he began to be sorrowful and troubled. Then he said to them, 'My soul is overwhelmed with sorrow to the point of death. Stay here and keep watch with me.'

Sitting still in silence with God can be very daunting if we are not used to it. I have found that St Teresa of Avila, who struggled for many years to concentrate the mind during prayer, has some useful suggestions that can help us focus on God in the quiet.

Lighting a candle makes a physical sign that the time of quiet has begun. It gives the eye something to concentrate upon and stills the mind.

Using an icon may seem off-beam to those in the evangelical or charismatic tradition, but when Christ seems far off, using a picture of Christ can help focus the mind on him and all he has done and longs to do for us.

My favourite suggestion of hers is to imagine Christ's presence. St Teresa used to keep Christ company in prayer in the garden of Gethsemane because, 'It seemed to me that his being alone and afflicted like a person in need made it possible for me to approach him.' Unlike the hard work of mental prayer, laying our needs before God, this is 'the prayer of quiet' in which the Lord gives us his peace through his presence.

Find some time and space to be comfortable, quiet and unhurried before God. Read today's passage in its entirety. Imagine the scene: it is dark, you are approaching the garden, enter and locate where Jesus is kneeling in prayer. How close do you feel you can get before you kneel and keep watch with him? Are you able to move closer the longer you are there? What do Christ's words of prayer make you feel? How do you respond? What is God speaking into your heart?

AS

FRIDAY 2 OCTOBER   Song of Solomon 2:10–13 (NRSV)
Sound the retreat

My beloved speaks and says to me: 'Arise, my love, my fair one, and come away.'

Eventually, if you catch the 'solitude' bug, there will come a time when you may want to get away from all the noise and crowdedness of the family home and see if you can cope with 'real' solitude and silence in a retreat house.

I grabbed my chance a week before Samuel was born and went on a 48-hour silent, guided retreat led by a clergywoman friend of ours. My one desire was to get away with Jesus, the lover of my soul, and listen to what he had to say to me.

I was relieved when the silence actually began, as people were forced to stop commenting on my enormous pregnant shape! To begin with, silence was hard to adjust to, but by the next morning I knew that I and others were beginning to 'tune in'. I can only describe it as comparable to a spiritual detoxification unit, where all the stresses, strains, concerns and worries of everyday life were drained away and replaced by 'the silence of eternity, interpreted by love'.

One of the spiritual exercises we had to do was to fold a piece of A4 paper into six squares and draw on four of them a picture representing key stages in our spiritual journey until that moment. Square five was for 'what God is saying to you today' and the last square, a personal prayer for the future. My square for the present contained a bridal bouquet of Spirea blooms from the retreat house garden. God had spoken to me through the passage I've given for today and made some very real promises for Mark's and my future. When we give the Lord space to meet with us, he does so in a very special and personal way, and we return to secular life much refreshed.

Make time to retreat; it can even be done at home. Try the A4 paper exercise for yourself. Keep it somewhere safe but to hand, as a reminder of God's faithfulness.

AS

SATURDAY 3 OCTOBER Zephaniah 3:17 (NIV)

The voice of the heart

The Lord your God is with you, he is mighty to save. He will take great delight in you, he will quiet you with his love, he will rejoice over you with singing.

It is impossible to do justice to solitude and silence in just two weeks, but I hope this has whetted your appetite to try to experience God in new and deeper ways in your own situation.

I chose today's verse as a word of encouragement on which to end this section. Making time to be with God may seem an impossible task for many women in the busy lives they lead. Remember, God is on our side in this matter; he is with us, not against us. Often we are our own stumbling-blocks, thinking we have to achieve certain spiritual standards before we can have a deep experience of God. This is not the case. God will meet us right where we are if we give him the slightest chance.

Jesus was willing to redeem and save us, we are precious and of great concern to him. He longs to see us grow up in the love the Father offers us. It is the realization of God's love that will lead us gently into those quiet places where we can meet with him. The Lord will show us where and when to stop and rest (Psalm 139, LB). If we do draw aside, we will hear in our hearts the Lord rejoicing over us with singing, like a bridegroom rejoices over his bride (Isaiah 62:5).

I would be a liar if I denied that prayer can be dry and arduous at times, but even the difficult times count as an unseen benefit to our souls and are not to be despised in the light of eternity.

'It is love which is the voice of the heart. Love God and you will always be speaking to him. The seed of love is growth in prayer ... Ask God to open your heart and kindle in it a spark of his love, then you will begin to understand what praying means.'
JEAN-NICHOLAS GROU (1730–1803)

AS

SUNDAY 4 OCTOBER · Psalm 16:1–2 (NIV)

Cheshire wives

Keep me safe, O God, for in you I take refuge. I said to the Lord, 'You are my Lord; apart from you I have no good thing.'

Several years ago my husband's job was transferred from London to Manchester. I gave up a well-paid job to move with him. Months of job-hunting failed: I was unable to find new work. The awkward dent this made in family finances was worsened by the fact that, for various reasons, we had bought a small house in the 'golden triangle' of north Cheshire, where there are more Rolls-Royces, private swimming pools and champagne parties than anywhere else in the country. £600,000 homes are common, and brochures in the waiting-area of our local bistro are entitled: 'Choosing your *next* yacht'.

Needless to say, my identity as a middle-class professional began to slip away. My earning power and former 'network' were gone. Compared to the local Cheshire wives, who fly to New York to shop, I felt like a peasant. Soon, a total failure.

It was then that I discovered these verses. Lonely, depressed, socially bewildered, desperate for work, I found this psalm expressed my prayer to God perfectly: 'Keep me safe [from stabs of envy, of despair] for in you I take refuge.'

I began to re-evaluate my life. I had lost most things, at a time when I lived in the midst of incredible materialism. Would I start longing for such luxury? I looked at the big houses, rolling acres, thoroughbred horses, Land Rovers, and expensive clothes all around me, and could certainly agree with the psalmist: 'I have no good thing.'

But, over the months, the words 'You are my Lord' became increasingly real to me. I had him. I discovered that his very real presence with me was more than enough, and that in fact the Lord had *always* been the only really 'good thing' I possessed.

A Ugandan refugee has put it this way: 'I never realized that Jesus was all I needed—until Jesus was all I had.' He is our refuge indeed.

AC

MONDAY 5 OCTOBER — Psalm 16:3 (NIV)

Best of friends

As for the saints who are in the land, they are the glorious ones in whom is all my delight.

Life is made up of relationships. When you think back over your Christian life, who were the special people whom God sent your way, just when you needed them most? Who helped you to find God in the first place? Who helped you in times of trouble? Who passed on great spiritual truths? And who 'blessed' you, leaving you nearer to God, simply through their love, kindness, mercy, humility and courage?

Our fellow Christians, of course, are the 'saints' referred to in the Bible. 'Saint' is literally 'holy one', a person of God. The New Testament used it of people who had been born again, of the Holy Spirit. That was the reason for their holiness; they were not 'holy' on their own.

'They are the glorious ones.' Our special Christian friends may look very ordinary, but when they talk about their faith, there is an inner radiance, a hint of future glory.

'In whom is all my delight.' I took other Christians for granted—until I moved to an area where I hardly ever met one. Within months it became a real *pleasure* to spend time with another Christian. I joined a prayer group of four women in the next village. They lead normal, everyday lives: busy husbands, young children. But in this materialistically wealthy area, they are my *true* wealth: a constant source of encouragement, laughter and companionship. Whenever the five of us are gathered together in Mary's living-room, we know that he is there in the midst of us, never mind the Barbies on the floor. Some groups of 'girlfriends' just meet and gossip. Not our group. Mary tells us that whenever she baby-sits, she prays her way around the family's house, asking God's blessing on the lives that are led in each of the rooms.

People whose love for God infuses their love for others—how can one not delight in them?

AC

TUESDAY 6 OCTOBER   Psalm 16:4 (NIV)
Modern gods

The sorrows of those will increase who run after other gods. I will not pour out their libations of blood or take up their names on my lips.

Money. Sex. Power. These are the names of some of the best-known gods of today. Millions of people serve them faithfully, and end by sacrificing their health, their marriages, their children, their very lives.

Money. We all want lots; we all need at least a little! But for some people, the desire to be rich, *really rich*, becomes an all-consuming passion. A novel by Tom Wolfe, *Bonfire of the Vanities*, tells the story of a New York stockbroker in the boom time of the 1980s who modestly considers himself a 'Master of the Universe'. He makes 'big bucks'—nearly £1 million a year—and craves even more. But money is not a kind god, and his life in the fast lane soon skids out of control.

Sex. A very popular modern god! But women who use their sexual attractiveness in an attempt to win romance and 'true love' are perhaps the saddest of people. The mother of a friend of mine decided to go looking for 'love', and became very promiscuous. It ended her marriage and alienated her children. As the years went by, she collected 'boyfriends' the way other women collect little pottery owls. But none ever kept her desire for 'real romance and true love' satisfied for long. Now seventy-two, she is still obsessed with the idea that out there somewhere is her Prince Charming who will make everything 'all right'. Of course, he isn't, and even if he was, he wouldn't.

Power. You might get it, if you are ambitious and ruthless enough, but how long can you hang on to it? Ask any politician after he's been voted out of office.

Money, sex, power. Three demanding, pitiless gods who devour your energies. Perhaps that is why the early Christians opted for poverty, chastity, obedience. And found contentment and peace.

AC

WEDNESDAY 7 OCTOBER   Psalm 16:5–6 (NIV)

This one's for you

Lord, you have assigned me my portion and my cup ... surely I have a delightful inheritance.

What gifts has God given you? Are you content with them, or do you fidget, wanting to go back and exchange them for something better?

This verse reminds me of the film *Amadeus*, which came out several years ago now. It tells the story of Mozart through the eyes of Antonio Salieri, another court composer. Salieri was a devout Catholic, and recognized that his music came ultimately from God. After finishing each composition, he would offer a prayer of thanksgiving to the little crucifix on his wall. He was well content, enjoying using the musical gift that God had given him.

Then the young genius, Mozart, arrives. His vulgarity appals Salieri, just as his dazzling talent astounds him—and throws him into despair. Salieri is stricken to the heart, and feels betrayed by God. How can such divine genius be given to a man of such crass manners and desires? He has always acknowledged the Saviour, yet he knows he will never write music like Mozart's. Salieri throws the crucifix into the fire, and begins his descent into bitter envy, destruction and madness. It is a very sad story, but understandable. Saleri's grief will be understood by anyone who has given all they have to something, and known that it is still not enough—that they will never scale the heights.

Poor Salieri. Without realizing it, he had begun thinking of God as an aid to his musical talent, rather than as his creator who could be loved for himself alone. No wonder he felt betrayed, instead of blessed, by God. Sadly, Salieri's passionate desire for musical genius gnawed away at him until it devoured even the talent he did have.

Spend a few minutes today counting your blessings. Ask God for the grace to be able to enjoy other people's talents and contributions without needing to match or better them. The gift is not the main thing; it is the giver. We can all enjoy him. And that is the best gift of all.

AC

THURSDAY 8 OCTOBER   Psalm 16:7–8 (NIV)
What's your advice?

I will praise the Lord, who counsels me; even at night my heart instructs me. I have set the Lord always before me. Because he is at my right hand, I shall not be shaken.

Everybody wants advice. Maybe not from our mothers, or even friends, but from someone, somewhere. If you doubt this, look at the cover of any woman's magazine. They thrive by offering their readers 'five tips for this', 'ten handy hints for that', and 'what to do when your husband does whatever'. We all have problems. We all want solutions.

Sometimes any array of 'experts' isn't enough. People in trouble long for more than self-medication: they want specific guidance and a cure. This may be the age of 'choices', but horoscopes—with direct advice and warnings—are more popular than ever. We seem to crave a 'divine' perspective on life, that says, 'This is right for you specifically at this time.'

Here's where Christians win hands down—because our God is a most personal, loving heavenly Father. He told us to think of him as Abba, or Daddy. He knows us: the Bible says he has called each one of us by name, and that even the hairs of our head are numbered. He wants us to know him, to 'abide' in him, to 'pray without ceasing', and he delights to guide us: 'If any of you is lacking in wisdom, ask God, who gives to all generously' (James 1:5, NRSV).

Hence these delightful lines from the psalmist, with their heart-warming glimpse into what real prayer can be—a constant referral of our daily lives to our Father, and a quiet certainty that he is there for us, guiding and guarding us. The psalmist mentions nights. We have all had sleepless nights, and sometimes those hours of darkness and solitude can be a time when fear, worry and regrets seep in around every corner of our mind and threaten to drown us in depair. But next time you lie awake, purposefully turn your thoughts towards God. Recite a verse or two. Set the Lord before you, and you will not be shaken.

AC

FRIDAY 9 OCTOBER   Psalm 16:9–10 (NIV)

Happy ever after

Therefore my heart is glad and my tongue rejoices; my body also will rest secure, because you will not abandon me to the grave, nor will you let your Holy One [or 'faithful one'] see decay.

Jane, a girl at my prayer group, had a friend who developed breast cancer in her late thirties. After a long struggle of some months, it became clear she was going to die. Jane was distraught, and prayed and prayed for her. Then one night she went to bed and had a most vivid dream. In the dream she saw her friend who had been so ill running across a great green open space, laughing and radiant. A great golden light suffused the whole landscape. Jane woke up, overwhelmed with the feelings of joy and sheer vitality that the dream had evoked. The powerful feelings that the dream had stirred up were still with her next morning.

Tentatively, Jane rang the family. She learned that her friend had died at exactly the same time as she had had the dream. Jane was awed, and felt that somehow she had been given a glimpse of her friend just arriving in eternity, with all the pain and grief gone for ever.

I was reminded of her experience when I read these words: 'My heart is glad ... you will not abandon me to the grave.' The psalmist could enjoy his life here and now because he was no longer frightened of death. Death had no 'sting', the grave no 'victory' over him.

It all goes along with Paul's triumphant declaration: 'For me to live is Christ, to die is gain.' And it will be our gain, too, some day. Jesus told his disciples that in his 'Father's house' was plenty of room, and that he was going away 'to prepare a place' for them. Then he would come back, and take them 'to be with me'.

Jesus will not let us see decay. When we die, we too will go to his Father's house, so that 'where I am', 'you also may be'.

AC

SATURDAY 10 OCTOBER   Psalm 16:11 (NIV)
Better than the Internet

You have made known to me the path of life; you will fill me with joy in your presence, with eternal pleasures at your right hand.

Some people have the most peculiar ideas about Christianity. I was at a dinner party the other evening and the subject of religion came up. One lonely woman admired Judaism for its stress on 'community'. Another, who'd had a stillborn son, thought some pagan practices in South America wonderful for their 'care' of the spirits of the dead. One of the men, whose job was insecure, argued that Eastern fatalism is the only sensible approach to life.

'Well,' I began, 'I'm a Christian...' and got no further. They turned on me in polite derision. 'Oh, you're not! How can you abide a God so good? It isn't natural,' said one woman. 'A God who judges and sends you to hell is disgusting,' the man growled. 'Don't ruin your life on a guilt trip. Enjoy it!' was the general consensus.

I thought about that conversation later. It struck me that all of them longed for a god who would be good to them, fulfil their needs, or at least help them to make sense of life. Yet none of them had dreamed of turning to Christianity. What has gone wrong?

Has the Christian Church failed to proclaim that Emmanuel is literally just that—God with us, loving us as we are, and through his death redeeming us if we repent? Or do some people simply prefer a god who operates more like the Internet? From whom they can download the odd bit of wisdom and comfort to empower them— but who leaves all the choices to them?

Sadly, these verses would not make sense to such people. Yet they shine with God's love for us. God has given us our five physical senses, through which comes all our enjoyment of life on earth; he guides us towards the path of life, and he promises that eternity will dazzle us with joy.

Love, joy and pleasure. All of these are ours because of Emmanuel.

AC

SUNDAY 11 OCTOBER Psalm 142:1–2 (NIV)

Why me?

I cry aloud to the Lord; I lift up my voice to the Lord for mercy. I pour out my complaint before him; before him I tell my trouble.

An old saying goes, 'There are only two certainties in life: death—and taxes.' I'd like to name a third: trouble. Illness, broken families, stressed jobs, debt, poverty, war—the possibilities are really endless.

If you think about it, it is understandable. For what would it take to make and keep anyone permanently, completely happy? Perfect childhood, health, looks, family, friends, colleagues, job (or no need to work at all!)? In a fallible world where we humans are so bound up together, and dependent upon each other, and yet retain our free will, it is only a wonder that there aren't more riots in the streets!

So the psalmist, David, does not wear himself out with wondering why trouble should have come to him in the first place. He accepts it as part of life. In his case he is being chased across an arid wilderness by King Saul and his soldiers, and is hiding in a cave. His devotion to God has not prevented their desire to kill him—in fact it is God's choice of him as the future king that has landed him in this trouble! Had God not shown such an interest in this shepherd boy, no one else would have bothered, either.

What do you do when you're in trouble? Does it come as a shock, as you're a Christian, and expect God only to bless you? Do you feel like reproaching God with a 'Hey, I'm on your side, remember?'—especially when you are trying to do the right thing? Well, it was the disciples, not the Pharisees, whom Jesus warned to expect tribulation in this world.

So what difference does being a Christian make? Like David, we have someone to turn to, someone who knows what is going on, and who cares about us. Everyone finds that the odds of life are stacked against them from time to time. But only Christians can bring God into the equation and ask for his help. Like David did.

AC

MONDAY 12 OCTOBER   Psalm 142:3–4 (NIV)
Out of Africa

When my spirit grows faint within me, it is you who know my way. In the path where I walk men have hidden a snare for me. Look to my right and see; no one is concerned for me. I have no refuge; no one cares for my life.

A friend of mine married an African twenty years ago and went off to live in Africa. It was a hard life, but she loved him, and accepted the violent city, the small house crowded with relatives, the poor food and the malaria. She struggled to bring up their four sons as well as she could. Then she discovered that her husband had become promiscuous. He was furious when she wanted to leave with the boys, and in his country he had the legal right to stop her. She was trapped. It was then that these verses might have been written by her.

She felt utterly alone, and desperate. No one would help her against him. So she spent days in silent prayer, casting herself upon God's mercy. Then the glimmerings of an escape plan began to take form. She prayed all one night, and by morning felt a wonderful, divine reassurance steal over her. She hid the boys' jumpers in bags beneath swimsuits and towels, and told her husband she was taking them to the swimming-pool that day. She reached for his hand in one last mute appeal, but he snatched it away. So she looked into his eyes and bade him silent farewell. His brother dropped her off at the swimming pool. She walked the boys in the front door ... and out the side door ... on to visit the British consul, who had just returned from England that morning. He got her a lift on an oil company's plane as far as the international airport. Then friends she ran into by 'chance' hid her for two days until her flight was called. Another friend paid the airfares.

She arrived in England in February with her young sons in jumpers, swimsuits and shorts. They were penniless. But they were safe. She knew God had found a way out for her.

AC

TUESDAY 13 OCTOBER   Psalm 142:5–6 (NIV)

God opens a door

I cry to you, O Lord; I say, 'You are my refuge, my portion in the land of the living.' Listen to my cry, for I am in desperate need; rescue me from those who pursue me, for they are too strong for me.'

Following on from yesterday's story, my friend arrived in England thinking she and the boys were safe. She soon discovered that international law would oblige Britain to return her boys at once to Africa if her husband so requested during their first year of separation. Meanwhile, she was penniless and homeless, with children wholly dependent on her.

The story of the following twelve months is anything but dull. From the depths of dismay, fear and bewilderment, she doggedly set about building a new life. She cried out daily to God, her only refuge. A series of doors began to open out of what had seemed blank, forbidding walls. Christians took her in, and housed her and the boys. Soon a little home of her own was found. She began a course in computer studies, which by a happy quirk in regulations she was able to turn into a master's degree. But month after month she and her solicitor waited, dreading a summons from the Foreign Office. Her new life in England would be barren and bitter if her sons were taken from her.

But no summons came. Her husband was mysteriously silent, other than sending her private letters demanding her return with the sons. Finally the mystery was solved: through friends in Africa she learned that her husband had told everyone she had left suddenly for health reasons, and he was happy for the boys to live in England. He was simply too proud to admit to the authorities that his wife had outsmarted him.

Meanwhile, my friend has just landed a good job in computing. Her boss turns out to be a Christian, and wants to sponsor her doctorate in due course.

Not all of us flee Africa destitute, but God can still rescue us and be our refuge if we call on him.

AC

WEDNESDAY 14 OCTOBER

Psalm 142:7 (NIV)

From prison to praise

Set me free from my prison, that I may praise your name. Then the righteous will gather about me because of your goodness to me.

A good few years ago there was a burglar in the East End of London named Fred Lemon. He had a violent temper, drank too much, and was in no way a 'New Man'. In fact, he had tried to strangle his own wife three times. Eventually he was arrested when he broke into a house, bumped into the owner and beat him nearly to death. Fred was sentenced to five years in Dartmoor. His wife didn't know whether to laugh or cry.

Fred was actually locked up in more than one kind of prison. Life in Dartmoor was miserable, but the shackles on his mind were far tighter, far more painful. The chaplain tried to help, but Fred raged and roared.

Then one night he had a vision. Jesus came into his cell and spoke to him. Now Fred was not a very imaginative character, but to his dying day he maintained he had had this vision. In any case, it shook him up so thoroughly that the next morning he walked free from the prison of his past childhood, his anger, his bitterness and his violence. The chaplain and wardens were dumbfounded. They had never seen anyone change so completely, so fast.

By the time Fred left Dartmoor he was a thoroughly informed—and growing—Christian. He apologized to his wife, opened a fruit and veg shop ... and then went back to prison—to preach. Over the next twenty years he worked his way up and down the prisons of England, an enthusiastic and unstoppable prison evangelist. Jesus had released him from his internal prison, and for the next twenty years he praised his name. The righteous did indeed gather around him—he was the first ever 'ex-con' to be invited to join the Christian Police Association!

Has God ever set you free from a particular prison? Did you remember to thank him?

AC

THURSDAY 15 OCTOBER   *Psalm 131:1 (NIV)*

Don't dream too big

My heart is not proud, O Lord, my eyes are not haughty; I do not concern myself with great matters or things too wonderful for me.

Psalm 131 is a beautiful little poem of the kind known as a psalm of confidence, or trust. Certainly the poem shines with simple holiness—and a great deal of common sense!

This poet recognizes his place in the scheme of things, and is content. The commentaries say that the Hebrew would be better translated, roughly, as, 'My life does not revolve around ambitions and schemes which are impossible.'

If you've ever been close to someone who is full of ambition and schemes that never succeed, you'll appreciate the wisdom of this particular psalm. You'll only wish that your loved one did, too!

I knew someone whose father was a highly educated professional in a senior position, when one day he decided he was bored and meant for better things. He decided to launch his own company from scratch. His wife was appalled, but he had a will of iron. He sold their comfortable home, and moved his family into a two-room flat so that he could plunge the cash into this new venture. He had no experience and no contacts in the new field. Nothing but towering confidence in himself as a gigantic success.

The big vision fizzed out, a bit like an exploding rocket. The company went up—and came right down again. The family lost even the two-room flat, and ended up in a friend's spare bedroom. Then the man had a heart attack and died, leaving his wife destitute.

This man's fall was more spectacular than most, but pride and selfish ambition can tempt anyone. We all have to make decisions in our lives that will affect other people. On what do you base your decisions? The psalmist knew that when we examine our motives carefully in the light of eternity, pride and selfishness will be seen for what they are.

AC

FRIDAY 16 OCTOBER *Psalm 131:2 (NIV)*

Are you stressed out?

But I have stilled and quietened my soul; like a weaned child with its mother, like a weaned child is my soul within me.

What a lovely image! A mother hushing and soothing a fractious, crying child until it settles in her arms, contented and at peace. The psalmist speaks of his soul as if it is a separate entity to himself, but this differentiation is for poetical purposes only.

Many people caught up in the frenetic rush of modern life know what it is to have a fractious 'soul'. The constant hammering of high expectations, too little time and fierce competition drives in the stress, fear and tension. Your anxious thoughts go round and round, and soon you can't sleep. A 'fractious soul' in perpetual overdrive can drive you as crazy as a child who won't stop screaming. Desperate mothers can become violent; no wonder people give way to burn-out and road rage.

The psalmist has taken positive action to still and quiet his soul. Anyone who has tried meditation will know what he means. Certainly millions of people turn to it, inside and out of Christianity. They are unable to bear their frenetic, anxious souls any longer. They want to hush them, quiet and soothe them.

There is a problem, however. When small children are fretful and 'mithering', as the northerners say, it is no good telling them to console themselves, and pull themselves together. They are truly upset, and need comfort and soothing from a loving, outside source. They need someone tangible to cling to. Our souls need the same thing. So non-Christians have a bit of an uphill struggle ahead of them when they meditate and try to still their souls. Their soul may subside for a while, but it is quite likely to suddenly demand: 'Don't tell me "Hush hush, now!" Give me one good reason *not* to panic!'

God is our loving heavenly Father. The Bible promises: 'You will keep in perfect peace him whose mind is steadfast, because he trusts in you' (Isaiah 26:3).

AC

SATURDAY 17 OCTOBER   *Psalm 131:3 (NIV)*

Not an emergency service

O Israel, put your hope in the Lord both now and for evermore.

Short verse, but long history behind it. It's like when you're out with a married couple who've survived very stormy times. The husband makes a sad little comment which means nothing much to anybody. But his wife slips him a rueful, embarrassed glance, and it is obvious that he is recalling some incident between them, and that there is a long story behind it all.

There was a very long, very turbulent story behind these few words. Many generations before, the Lord had rescued Israel out of slavery in Egypt, and made a covenant with her in the Sinai desert. He would be her God, and she would be his chosen people. He then led her across the wilderness, fed her with manna, and helped her take possession of the promised land. Israel had eagerly accepted all his help—and had then become unfaithful to him. As the years went by, Israel sampled every other god going, from golden calves to lumps of wood, from Baal to Asherah poles—you name it, she'd worship it.

It was crazy, really. When the Lord blessed Israel, she went her own sweet way, taking it all for granted. When he thundered at her, she jumped in fright and dismay, and would promise she'd never do it again. Many marriages operate along similar lines, for the same reason: one of the partner's heart is, deep down, not really in it. They are terminally self-centred, and take their spouse's goodwill for granted. Occasionally remorse sets in, when they realize they've gone too far and a fuss is going to be made; but rarely repentance.

Sadly, this describes many people's relationship with God today. They use God as the fourth member of the emergency services. They 'hope' in God only when all else fails. Like the sick man who heard people at church were praying for him, and quavered, 'Oh dear, am I as bad as that?!'

The 'hope' here translates also as 'confidence' and 'security'. God offers us all this, both now and for evermore. Make the most of it.

AC

SUNDAY 18 OCTOBER   Luke 1:1–4 (RSV)

Telling the stories

It seemed good to me also, having followed all things closely for some time past, to write an orderly account for you, most excellent Theophilus, that you may know the truth concerning the things of which you have been informed.

Luke begins his great gospel with an explanation of what he is writing, a mention of who he is writing for, and his reason for writing. His intention is to write a clear and detailed account of all the things that he has heard about Jesus, in order to give his friend an accurate picture.

Tradition has it that Luke was a doctor, which would help to explain his interest in people and their various conditions. There are more stories about Jesus healing diseases in Luke than in any of the other gospels, and also more about the women around Jesus. Luke probably talked to Mary, Jesus' mother, as well as to Mark, to find out as much as he could about what Jesus said and did.

The picture that emerges of Jesus in Luke's gospel is of a real human with a deep love and compassion for other people, especially those who were poor, needy, ill or knew themselves to be sinners. In addition, Luke stressed the fact that Jesus was more than just a good man: he was also the Saviour. In a sense, we follow in Luke's tradition when we talk to other Christians or read about what they have learnt about Jesus. Of course, we are separated from those who knew Jesus by more than just a few years, but we can still add to the ever-growing witness to our Lord by sharing our stories with other believers.

When you tell someone about who Jesus was and what he did, and also about what he means to you, you are taking part in spreading the good news of Jesus Christ. In short, you are telling your own gospel!

Dear Lord, please help me to think about what you did on earth, as well as to think about what you have done for me. And then, help me to tell the people I meet about you. Amen.
Read John 20:24–31

CR

MONDAY 19 OCTOBER Luke 1:6–7 (RSV)

Our flawed reality

And they were both righteous before God, walking in all the commandments and ordinances of the Lord blameless. But they had no child, because Elizabeth was barren, and both were advanced in years.

Before Luke begins his story about the life of Jesus, he writes about the circumstances surrounding the birth of John the Baptist. John's parents were Zechariah, a priest, and Elizabeth, a woman descended from Aaron and related to Mary, Jesus' mother. Luke describes Zechariah and Elizabeth in a way that most of us would probably love to be described, as righteous and obedient people.

And yet there was a great sadness in the lives of this virtuous couple: they had no children. What is more, Elizabeth was barren and had passed her child-bearing years. In human terms their situation was hopeless.

I would like to make two observations on this passage. First, Elizabeth's childlessness was not a result of divine punishment for any sin in her life. It was a tragic but not uncommon condition that has affected many women throughout history, right up to the present. Second, the fact of their childlessness had not made Elizabeth and Zechariah bitter or resentful towards God.

Our problem may not be infertility, but most of us have circumstances or conditions in our lives that seem both unfair and beyond help. We must not let these become either reasons to doubt God's love for us or excuses to blame God. Nor should they drive us to imagine that there must be some hidden sin in our lives for which God is holding us accountable.

Sometimes things are the way they are simply because we live in an imperfect and fallen world. The challenge is to accept our present reality, while always holding up ourselves and others to the mercy and transforming power of God's Holy Spirit.

O God, grant us the serenity to accept what cannot be changed, the courage to change what can be changed, and the wisdom to know the difference. (Reinhold Niebuhr)
Read Romans 8:18–28

CR

TUESDAY 20 OCTOBER
Luke 1:13 (RSV)

Your prayer is heard

But the angel said to him, 'Do not be afraid, Zechariah, for your prayer is heard, and your wife Elizabeth will bear you a son, and you shall call his name John.'

Not long ago the phone rang, and the chirpy voice on the other end told me that I had won a £500 holiday voucher. My immediate response was to ask repeatedly if the caller was genuine. She assured me that she was. Gradually, I began to believe that I might have won the competition. Then she told me of a product that I would first have to view in order to receive the holiday voucher. My suspicions returned, but we agreed a day to meet. The time came and went, but no one arrived. When I phoned the company to set up a new time, a recorded message said that the number was unobtainable. It *had* been too good to be true.

In that instance, my scepticism was well founded, and I should never have allowed myself to hope that the caller was genuine. Sadly, many of us approach God with the same attitude of caution and suspicion!

When at last Zechariah was promised that Elizabeth would become pregnant and have a baby, his immediate response was much like mine to the mystery caller. He didn't believe it!

Whether or not our prayers are answered in the way we expect, we can have confidence that God hears our prayers. After all, the aim of our prayers is not to dictate to God what we want him to do for us, but to draw closer to him in an attitude of trust and openness. In such an attitude we will be in a better position to receive all that God has for us.

Lord, please help us to trust your love for us so much that we are able to accept whatever you have for us, no matter how unlikely it seems. And help us to believe that you do want to satisfy the deep desires of our hearts. Amen.
Read Psalm 139:1–18.

CR

WEDNESDAY 21 OCTOBER *Luke 1:14 (RSV)*

Accepting joy

And you will have joy and gladness, and many will rejoice at his birth.

The angel Gabriel tells Zechariah that Elizabeth will have a baby, what name they are to give him, and also what his purpose in life will be. Their son John, as yet unborn, will help to prepare people for the coming of the Messiah. What an extraordinary message!

Along with the amazing role John was to fulfil, Gabriel stressed something else: the birth would bring great joy. In fact, joy was the keynote of Luke's story of the births of both John and Jesus.

It is important to remember that Luke spoke of this joy even though he knew what was to happen later to both John and Jesus. He could have given the angel's words a tragic, or even a sinister, twist. He could have hinted that there were rocky times ahead. But Luke wrote of joy and gladness.

Even with the benefit of hindsight, the verdict was joy. Even taking into account the suffering and heart-rending deaths that were to come, Luke emphasized joy. The overwhelming joy of the good news that John was to point to, and that Jesus was to bring, put their own deaths into perspective.

Some of us tend to be so cautious, so careful not to be too joyous, too abandoned to God, because we know that life cannot be lived on a permanent high. We know that life brings sadness and heartbreak as well as joy. But the message of God's love is that, even in the middle of the hard times, we can know that God is with us.

The message of God's love and saving grace is ultimately more powerful than anything that can ever happen to us. None of us knows the future, but, whatever it turns out to be, we can know that the good news of Jesus Christ overarches everything.

Lord of joy, help me to believe that your love for me is real, and that nothing is stronger than your love. Amen.
Read Hebrews 12:1–2.

CR

THURSDAY 22 OCTOBER   Luke 1:19 (RSV)

Angels

And the angel answered him, 'I am Gabriel, who stand in the presence of God; and I was sent to speak to you, and to bring you this good news.'

I have sometimes felt that westerners in the twentieth century are operating at a disadvantage. We don't seem to have much visual evidence of God around us, and we don't get visited by angels at the important moments of our lives. Or do we?

When I was little, my mother taught me that angels were real, and that God made sure that there was always an angel or two watching over me. I was not to pray to the angels directly, or ever expect to see them, but I would know they were there.

Later on, I heard wonderful stories of ordinary-looking people turning up suddenly to help people in times of great need. Mysteriously, they would vanish just as suddenly, after they had done their work. More recently, I have read about people who claim that angels are everywhere, helping people in many different ways and sending messages that it is possible for us to receive. At times, I have found myself praying that God would send some of his angels to protect me and my family and friends.

Certainly, the Bible is full of references to angels, both in the Old and New Testaments, and, like Gabriel, they are often sent by God to communicate directly with people. At first, Zechariah was frightened when Gabriel came to him, but soon he was talking to Gabriel and asking him for some proof that his words were true. I would like to think that if Gabriel had come to me with a message from God, I would have believed him!

I believe that there are angelic beings, created by God for purposes we don't fully understand. And if God has created them, then we can be thankful for them, whether or not we ever see one.

Lord of the universe, protect us, we pray, and help us to receive all those whom you send. Amen.
Read Psalm 91.

CR

FRIDAY 23 OCTOBER   *Luke 1:22 (RSV)*

Unbelief makes us dumb

And when he came out, he could not speak to them, and they perceived that he had seen a vision in the temple; and he made signs to them and remained dumb.

Zechariah lost his power of speech because he did not believe what the angel Gabriel had been sent to tell him. He challenged Gabriel and began to argue that it would be impossible for his wife to have a baby. I can almost hear Zechariah reacting to Gabriel's message in the tones of Victor Meldrew of *One Foot in the Grave*: 'I don't believe it!'

Gabriel responded by declaring that Zechariah would be struck dumb until the promised event had happened. In fact, Zechariah remained dumb until eight days after the baby was born, when he wrote on a tablet that the boy's name was to be John, showing that he had accepted what the angel had said.

Zechariah's condition must have mystified his friends and his wife, but it gave him a constant and unavoidable reminder of his encounter with the angel. For nine long months Zechariah would have been able to think about his angelic visitor and what it all meant.

I am certain that God speaks to us by his Holy Spirit through his word, through other people and circumstances, and to our own spirits. I am also certain that we ignore much of what God is saying to us. It would be so much easier if God could hit each of us over the head with a rubber mallet whenever he wanted to get a really important message through to us. But that's not how God behaves.

It takes a listening heart and spirit to hear what God is saying, and the continual exercise of placing and keeping ourselves in God's presence. What was physically true for Zechariah is spiritually true for us. If we discount what God is saying to us we become spiritually disabled and unable to move on. Thankfully, God is persistent and keeps on reaching out to us.

O Lord, help me to believe you. Amen.
Read Matthew 17:14–21.

CR

SATURDAY 24 OCTOBER *Luke 1:30 (RSV)*

Finding favour with God

And the angel said to her, 'Do not be afraid, Mary, for you have found favour with God.'

I have often wondered what it was about Mary that made God chose her. Was she specially holy, obedient and loving? Did she possess inner reserves of strength and patience? Was she extraordinarily wise or virtuous? Had God waited until Mary came along before he felt he could finally become one of the human race?

Clearly, Mary was a good and kind person, and yes, she was obedient and humble. Later on she also proved to be very strong. But was she so different from other faithful and loving people? Was the timing of the incarnation dependent upon Mary or upon other factors?

I believe God chose to become human at a time that was somehow right for him. He needed a human mother, and he chose Mary. However, I do not believe that the Messiah would not have been sent if Mary had not existed. If there had been no Mary, or if she had said no, God would still have sent us a saviour, but he would have been different.

When Gabriel was sent to Mary he greeted her by calling her, 'O favoured one', and he told her not to be afraid, saying that she had 'found favour with God'. More than two thousand years later, I ache to know just what she was like and why God settled on her. I read and reread the gospels, trying to piece together the life of this chosen woman. She seems to behave the way most dedicated, proud and conscientious mothers would behave.

Whatever Mary was really like, she was most certainly not the passive, frail young woman who appears on Christmas cards. She brought up her son, knowing that he was special, and then had to watch him die. She is worthy of our respect and gratitude.

Dear Lord, help us to be like Mary, yielded and obedient to you. Help us to live our lives so that, like Mary, we also find favour in your sight. Amen.
Read Colossians 3:12–17.

CR

SUNDAY 25 OCTOBER   Luke 1:37 (RSV)

God can do it

For with God nothing will be impossible.

Gabriel has just told Mary that she will have a baby and that her cousin Elizabeth is also pregnant. The angel then ends his message with the sweepingly expansive phrase, 'For with God nothing will be impossible.' It is a powerful, ringing statement, and I have heard it quoted many times. But just what did Gabriel mean?

Did he mean that God can do anything, even the things which seem impossible? In theory, this may be what he was stating, but in reality that is not our experience of how God works.

For instance, it may be possible for God to calm the violent winds and waves of a hurricane, but hurricanes still happen. It may be possible for God to stay a murderer's hand, but people are still killed. It may be possible for God to sustain the life of a dying child, but hundreds of thousands of children still die each year. Can God really do the impossible?

For reasons we do not fully understand, God has chosen to limit his power in our world. No doubt it has something to do with the Fall, and with not only humankind's but all of creation's separation from God. God does not step across the boundaries that our fallen world has created.

I think that what Gabriel meant was that nothing will ultimately stand in the way of God's will for his people. There may be obstacles along the way, but in the end God will see his purpose fulfilled for his creation. In that sense Gabriel was right, and one day the present world order will pass away, and then, with God, nothing will be impossible.

God is working his purpose out as year succeeds to year;
God is working his purpose out and the time is drawing near;
Nearer and nearer draws the time, the time that shall surely be,
When the earth shall be filled with the glory of God
as the waters cover the sea.
ARTHUR CAMPBELL AINGER (1841–1919)

Read Revelation 22:1–5.

CR

MONDAY 26 OCTOBER — Luke 1:38 (RSV)

Submission

And Mary said, 'Behold, I am the handmaid of the Lord; let it be to me according to your word.' And the angel departed from her.

For centuries Mary has been held up as the ideal woman: pure, holy, obedient and submissive. She has been presented as the ultimate role model for women, but she is one which, unfortunately, few women can hope to emulate. For starters, those of us who are mothers are not virgins, and her virginity was considered to be an important part of her character. In fact, so problematical has Mary been for Christian women, that some have rejected her as an example worthy of our attention.

However, my view is that those who have little regard for Mary are as misguided as those who venerate her as someone who is partially divine. Mary does present us with an excellent example, one to be followed by both women *and* men.

When Mary was presented with a frightening and difficult situation, she revealed a remarkably trusting and humble spirit. I find her acceptance of what God was asking of her both moving and inspiring. I doubt whether I would have responded so beautifully, and I can imagine myself making good, logical excuses to Gabriel.

Submission may have become an unpopular word in our society, but I think we all need to look again at this young woman and learn from her. Precisely because Mary was fully human and not divine, we can identify with her. Unlike her son, she was not perfect, but when it mattered she said 'yes' to God.

Our obedience to God may not have such earth-shattering repercussions, but every time we say 'yes' to God we help to usher in his kingdom and bring about his will for humankind. Thanks to Mary, the Son of God became one of us. I am certain that God still relies on our submission.

O Lord, we thank you for the example of your earthly mother, and we pray that we might learn true submission to your will. Amen.
Read 1 Samuel 15:22–23 and Luke 1:46–55.

CR

TUESDAY 27 OCTOBER   Luke 1:41–42 (RSV)

The Holy Spirit

And when Elizabeth heard the greeting of Mary, the babe leaped in her womb; and Elizabeth was filled with the Holy Spirit and she exclaimed with a loud cry, 'Blessed are you among women, and blessed is the fruit of your womb!'

Gabriel had told Zechariah that his son John would be filled with the Holy Spirit even from when he was in his mother's womb. Later, when Elizabeth is six months pregnant, the angel's words are fulfilled. As Mary enters her home and greets her, the baby leaps inside her.

Luke writes that not only did the baby respond to Mary's arrival in a special way, but also that Elizabeth herself was filled with the Holy Spirit and uttered a prophetic message.

In orthodox Christianity the Holy Spirit is recognized as one of the three persons who make up the Trinity. Yet many people seem uncomfortable with the Holy Spirit. The truth is, we owe all our faith and understanding of God to the Holy Spirit. It is the Spirit who shows us who God is, and the Spirit who lives in us and makes it possible for us to live as Jesus taught us to live. Wherever there is love, the Holy Spirit is at work. Wherever there is repentance, the Holy Spirit has been active. Wherever there are healings or miracles, or peace and unity, the Holy Spirit is present. As Christians we do not have to look outside us for the Spirit, because Jesus promised that the Spirit would come and live in us.

As the wind is thy symbol, so forward our goings.
As the dove, so launch us heavenwards.
As water, so purify our spirits.
As a cloud, so abate our temptations.
As dew, so revive our languor.
As fire, so purge out our dross.
CHRISTINA ROSSETTI

Read John 14:16–17 and 1 John 4.

CR

WEDNESDAY 28 OCTOBER — Luke 1:56 (RSV)

Time for friends

And Mary remained with her about three months, and returned to her home.

Last Christmas I was so busy that I didn't send cards to many of my friends. It made me feel guilty and hypocritical. I say I believe in the importance of keeping up with friends, and even that how in relating to each other we discover more of what it means to be human, as well as gaining insights into the nature of God. So much for my lofty thoughts and good intentions! That is why, when I read about Mary having spent three months with her cousin Elizabeth, it makes me pause. Who of us these days can afford to spend three days, let alone three months, with our friends or families?

Recently, my sister and brother-in-law who live abroad came for a two-day visit. They had given me about three weeks' notice of their trip. I had to cancel meetings and abandon hours of writing time. I found it depressing that my schedule was so full that seeing my own sister for a few days cost me time that I have had difficulty in making up. I know I am not alone in having an absurdly overcrowded diary. That experience made me think about what I really believe about friendship and time spent with other people. I have decided that I want more time for friendships, old ones as well as new ones, and I intend to make changes. For starters, I have talked to my husband, who is my closest friend, and we have pledged to go away at least once a quarter, even if only for a day or two. In addition, I plan to become a lady who lunches—at least once in a while! Further, I am steeling myself to say 'no' to certain invitations so that I can say 'yes' more often to having friends come to stay.

I know Mary had a very different lifestyle to the one most of us lead, but consider her son. He had only a few years to bring God's message of love and salvation, and yet he was never in a hurry. The years of his ministry are filled with stories of his encounters with people—people who, if they were alive today, I would probably be too busy even to notice.

Dear Lord, please give us your peace and your pace for our lives. Help us to take time to enjoy the people you have brought into our lives. Amen.
CR

THURSDAY 29 OCTOBER   Luke 1:62–63 (RSV)

Agreeing with God

And they made signs to his father, inquiring what he would have him called. And he asked for a writing tablet, and wrote, 'His name is John.' And they all marvelled.

For nine months Zechariah had been unable to speak. His disbelief when Gabriel had told him that he would become a father had resulted in his becoming dumb. Although Luke had described him as a righteous man, Zechariah became a man who doubted God. But when his son was born, and it was time to name the child, Zechariah showed that his disbelief had turned to belief.

By agreeing to name the baby the name that Elizabeth wanted, which was also the name that Gabriel had said the boy would be called, Zechariah was once again working with God, instead of doubting him. Immediately after writing the name on the tablet, Zechariah was able to speak again, and his first utterance was to bless God.

There are times when I feel the Lord is asking me to do something very small and unimportant, such as telephone a friend or do a certain errand at a certain time. Often it seems too trivial to be of interest to God, but when I have obeyed, I have known God's peace and joy, and sometimes also the reason why I was meant to act.

I like to think that when I agree with God and obey him, I am helping to spread his kingdom on earth. In a sense, God needs us to help him accomplish his purposes for his people. I also like to imagine that when each of us makes choices that agree with God's will, we are helping to add to a beautiful bright light that will one day cover the whole earth. Every time we speak up for God's way, or do an act of kindness, the light grows and the darkness is diminished.

Dear Lord, help me to accept what you have for me today and every day, knowing that your peace comes only when I am following you. Amen. Read 2 Corinthians 5:7–21.

CR

FRIDAY 30 OCTOBER   Luke 1:65 (RSV)

What would the neighbours say?

And fear came on all their neighbours. And all these things were talked about through all the hill country of Judea.

It's easy to picture: the dumb Zechariah suddenly speaking again after his wife produces a baby whom they both insist is to be called John. And this from an older couple who before then had never done anything to bring attention to themselves. No wonder the neighbours were talking!

Extravagant compliments excepted, I always find it somewhat disconcerting to hear from a third party what other people have been saying about me. First of all, I never imagine that I am ever the subject of gossip, so it always comes as a surprise to learn that others have been discussing some aspect of my life. But if gossip is a part of life for most if not all of us, then it might be worthwhile to consider what people might be saying about us.

Last summer my younger daughter sang in a pop group, which quite inexplicably shot to relative fame. Her picture was on the front of all the local papers, and she and the other girls in the band were frequent guests on radio stations. At the end of the summer she quit the band, opting to carry on with her studies.

For weeks afterwards, every time I went to the local shops I would be treated to a variety of opinions about my daughter and her decision, as well as confident suppositions about how I must have felt about it all!

We can't choose what opinions other people have of us, nor can we ensure that all our actions will be understood. But if people are going to talk about us, let's see if we can give them something really good to talk about, such as our generosity and hospitality, or our compassion and kindness. Wouldn't it be wonderful to have a reputation as someone who is always loving and understanding!

Lord, let me care more about your opinion of me, and let your love flow through me so freely that others are drawn to you. Amen.
Read John 4:1–29.

CR

SATURDAY 31 OCTOBER   *Luke 1:76 (RSV)*

Preparing the way

And you, child, will be called the prophet of the Most High; for you will go before the Lord to prepare his ways.

At the end of the story of John's birth, Luke writes that Zechariah is filled with the Holy Spirit and prophesies over his infant son. It is a beautiful passage, bringing promises of salvation for God's people from their enemies as well as from their sins. In it, Zechariah reiterates part of what the angel Gabriel first told him about his baby—namely, that he would go before the Christ to prepare the way for him.

We know nothing about the first thirty years of John's life, except that it was spent in the wilderness, after which he emerged to begin his public ministry. He soon attracted a group of disciples and spent his time teaching that the Messiah was coming and that people needed to repent and be cleansed of their sins. John also baptized people in the River Jordan, saying that his baptism of water was preparing them for the Messiah's baptism by the Spirit of God.

When Jesus came, John identified him as the Messiah and encouraged his own disciples to become followers of Jesus. He knew that his work was finished.

We might imagine that none of us now can ever have such an important work as John the Baptist, but Jesus made a startling statement: 'I tell you, among those born of women none is greater than John; yet he who is least in the kingdom of God is greater than he' (Luke 7:28). It is a humbling and challenging thought.

Dear God, thank you for the faithfulness of John the Baptist who pointed to Jesus as the Christ. Help us in our lives to point to Jesus as the one who came to show us who you are. Amen.
Read Matthew 3:1–17; Mark 1:1–15; Luke 3:1–22 or John 1:1–41.

CR

SUNDAY 1 NOVEMBER *Isaiah 66:12 (NIV)*

What is peace?

For this is what the Lord says [of Jerusalem, whose name means 'possession of peace']: 'I will extend peace to her like a river, and the wealth of nations like a flooding stream; you will nurse and be carried on her arm and dandled on her knees.'

What does the word 'peace' make you think of? Absence of war, conflict or anxiety? The relief when pain subsides or a baby stops crying? If you close your eyes, what do you see?

'I see a dove,' said my daughter, 'and I'm sitting by a stream, under a willow tree; there's music playing and everything's clean.' Great, unless it rains!

I see a river, wide and strong—probably because my subconscious registers choruses which draw on biblical imagery like the verse above. A river fits the biblical concept of peace, *shalom*, which is less about the absence of negatives than the presence of wholeness, well-being, completeness. That kind of peace is beyond our understanding because it flows out from God's very nature and, like a river, nothing can stop it. Strong and dynamic, it can be given and received, both by individuals who find inner peace in the most terrible circumstances and by communities, churches, cities, nations.

I must admit that my own experience of peace falls far short of that ideal and seems sometimes as fragile as a bubble. But God planned his kingdom of peace from the beginning. Though our selfishness and strife batter *shalom*, causing both God and mankind untold pain, his own peace remains as strong as eternity. We have always rebelled against God's reign of peace and love, but on the cross Jesus earned the right to rule again as prince of peace. In his new Jerusalem, his 'possession of peace', the most vulnerable will find wholeness, safety, love and utter security.

May your kingdom come, Lord, but until then, help me to swim in the river of your peace and to carry that peace to others. Amen.

CL

MONDAY 2 NOVEMBER   *Isaiah 54:10 (NIV)*

Losing our peace?

'Though the mountains be shaken and the hills be removed, yet my unfailing love for you will not be shaken nor my covenant of peace be removed,' says the Lord, who has compassion on you.

Here's me writing a series on peace and I'm a terrible worrier! A few years back, an appeal to get our son into an appropriate secondary school left me limp, and then, a few days off exchanging contracts on our new house, it seemed the move would fall through. I couldn't sleep, concentrate on anything else or pray. I 'handed the problems over to Jesus' several times an hour, but they sprang straight back like elastic, hitting me in the face. Even the kids complained, 'Mum's so stressed out!' For goodness sake, how long had I been a Christian? I despised myself as an utter failure.

On the school run I thought my head would burst with anxious thoughts churning round and round. To stop them, on the way home I sang every hymn and chorus I could think of, through gritted teeth (not a pretty sound!) Had I been God I'd have run a mile, but suddenly I felt his presence in the car.

'Do you really think I'm not big enough to cope with you?' he asked.

'But I can't even get my head in order, Lord,' I replied.

'No, and that's frightening you more than the uncertainties of the move. But listen, you're not a problem to me; nothing you could do would spin me into panic mode.'

Oh! He seemed to be smiling at me as a father might on rescuing a small child accidentally shut in a dark cupboard for all of ten seconds. 'It's all right,' he whispered, and it was as if his cool hand smoothed my burning forehead, 'you're all right!'

He urges us to trust him instead of becoming anxious and afraid—wise words to preserve our peace and well-being! But even if I blow all that completely, he won't disown me; his peace, infinitely bigger than mine, will keep me. 'You'll be all right,' he said, and I was!

Lord, will you be my peace, now and for ever! Amen.

CL

TUESDAY 3 NOVEMBER *Isaiah 60:17–21 (NIV)*

God's rule—peace and righteousness

Instead of bronze I will bring you gold, and silver in place of iron. Instead of wood I will bring you bronze, and iron in place of stones. I will make peace your governor and righteousness your ruler.

These words, prophesied to the Jews in exile, spoke of the splendid city God planned for them on their return. The RSV translates it, 'I will make your overseers peace and your taskmasters righteousness.' Isn't God good! What a contrast to the time when these same people were slaves building Egyptian pyramids.

Who else but God would choose peace to rule over us? Colossians 3:15 says, 'Let the peace of God rule in your hearts, since as members of one body you were called to peace.' The word 'rule' here applied to the one who arbitrated in the public games—the umpire or referee. I've often heard that verse used about personal guidance: 'I had no peace about that so I didn't do it.' In fact this verse, as well as the Isaiah passage, has a social context. Nor is righteousness restricted to personal clean living; its primary meaning concerns justice.

Peace and righteousness often go hand in hand, as in Romans 14:17: 'The kingdom of God is ... righteousness, peace and joy in the Holy Spirit.' This is the kind of society God wants, because that's what he's like—and he made us in his image. 'Blessed are those who hunger and thirst for righteousness,' said Jesus, 'for they will be filled ... Blessed are the peacemakers, for they will be called sons of God' (Matthew 5:6, 9).

These are big things, God. How can I help your peace and justice grow in the society in which I live? Help me to see the world around me in the way you see it and then to see things, little or big ones, which you're asking me to do. Give me the confidence to do them, in your name. But most of all thank you that you, the all-powerful, choose always to rule in righteousness and peace. Amen

CL

WEDNESDAY 4 NOVEMBER   Isaiah 26:1–4 (NIV)
Enemies of peace—double-mindedness

You will keep in perfect peace him whose mind is steadfast, because he trusts in you.

We know that on the one hand, 'there is no peace for the wicked' (Isaiah 57:21) and on the other, 'great peace have they who love your law, and nothing can make them stumble' (Psalm 119:165). But some of the unhappiest people I've known, the ones who suffer the worst excesses of lack of peace, are those who dither on the edge of God's kingdom. Perhaps they've followed Jesus in the past, even seen him work in amazing ways, but then something caused them to back off. All too often it's because they've been hurt by other Christians.

Jesus would welcome them back with great rejoicing, but they find it incredibly hard to recommit their love and trust to him. There again, because they've experienced his goodness and felt his power, they can't forget, stay away and enjoy their lives without him. Jesus said, 'A kingdom divided against itself will fall.' If the source of our true peace is in him and we, by his grace, gain access to that peace by living under his rule (in his kingdom), no wonder the double-minded tear themselves apart.

Yet there's hope. Peter followed Jesus for three years, seeing and doing amazing things. Yet after his Lord's arrest he hung around on the edge, dangerously near to Jesus but not close enough, until he found himself denying all he knew to be true. Later, after the risen Jesus reached out to him, we know that Peter went on to lead the Church, remaining steadfast to his Lord through life, church disputes, even martyrdom. God specializes in restoring peace, both to broken individuals who have betrayed him and to a broken world.

Do you know anyone 'on the edge'? Pray for them now and ask God to show you specific ways in which you can reach out to them with his compassion, trustworthiness and unconditional love. Pray also for yourself, your family and your church, that all may keep steadfastly trusting Jesus.

CL

THURSDAY 5 NOVEMBER   *Psalm 34:14 (NIV)*

Enemies of peace—drivenness

Seek peace and pursue it.

I told my hairdresser about our idyllic holiday when Scottish weather turned Mediterranean (really!) She said, 'I bet that's given you loads of ideas for new books!'

It hadn't. I felt guilty until I remembered the space and peace, the air and laughter. 'No, but it's recharged me!' I replied.

A successful young businesswoman on TV explained that she had no time for hobbies, a social life or enjoying her wealth. Extreme? A manic work ethic drives many Protestants, Catholics and atheists alike! We all know that mothers can *never* do enough. Elderly or disabled people need transport, the mothers' and toddlers' group needs helpers, the sick need visiting and the Alpha supper needs cooking.

Rousing sermons urge us to pray more, to support missionaries or the homeless, to get involved in the community or save the planet. All great in themselves, but … did *you* feel guilt rising as you read the list?

If we're driven by guilt or greed or legalism we'll drive ourselves into a mess and everyone else up the wall. In Jesus' story of the lost son, the older brother complained, 'All these years I've been slaving for you and never disobeyed your orders' (Luke 15:29). Resentment consumed him because, though his father's love and provision had always been there for him, he had never stopped to enjoy them.

After he created the world, God stopped to rest, not out of exhaustion but because he wanted to revel in his sense of well-being that everything was complete and good. What else is that but *shalom* peace? While hating joyless Sabbatarianism, sometimes I forget that God commanded us to rest because he rests. If we broke with our restless culture and obeyed him by seeking peace, maybe we'd stand out as different, more attractive, and we'd communicate well-being, not frenzy!

In the words of the song, 'Why don't you stop, and smell the roses?' Enjoy God, your family, friends, a good book … or just sit down and think beautiful thoughts!

CL

Friday 6 November — *Matthew 5:9 (NIV)*

Peacemakers

Blessed are the peacemakers, for they will be called sons of God.

A man told me he had led activity holidays successfully for thirty years until, last summer, one group became locked in acrimony. Letters of complaint flooded in. At first the leader puzzled over what had gone wrong; the group seemed normal at the beginning and he had done nothing different. However, one man had kept grumbling and stirring up trouble and it transpired that another holiday company had banned him for similar behaviour. One individual can spoil everything.

Conversely, in a job as a junior librarian I found the kind of staffroom jibes that plague all too many workplaces. Unfortunately some disparaging remarks about senior librarians contained truth. I tried to be reasonably positive and polite to everyone but never affected the atmosphere much. Then a new library assistant joined as our most junior member of staff. Though not a Christian, she had the sunniest of dispositions and her smile seemed to light up the place. Immediately popular, she treated everyone the same and found something good to say about each one, especially when negative comments were flying. If something went wrong she would laugh, not to put anyone down, but because she saw the funny side. If possible she would volunteer to help put it right, however much it inconvenienced her. Soon lunch breaks in the staffroom became enjoyable instead of something to be avoided at all costs and everyone started working as a team again.

She challenged me. Peacemaking on a macro scale is probably not for many. I'm unlikely to influence troubled areas like Northern Ireland, except through prayer. But anyone can promote peace among the people they meet day by day—and, let's face it, our churches, as well as the workplace and the school gate, need all the peacemakers they can get!

Lord, you gave your life to give us peace, so you know it's not always easy to be a peacemaker. Will you help me see specific ways in which I can pass on your gift of peace to the people I meet, not just now but every day? Amen.

CL

SATURDAY 7 NOVEMBER John 14:27 (NIV)

Knowing peace

Peace I leave with you; my peace I give you. I do not give to you as the world gives. Do not let your hearts be troubled and do not be afraid.

Peace? Was Jesus joking? His disciples were about to see their Lord tortured to death and afterwards would huddle together, terrified for their own safety. Later, as pioneers of the early Church their lives might be described as adventurous, but surely not as peaceful!

Paul's words give us a clue, 'Therefore, since we have been justified through faith, we have peace with God through our Lord Jesus Christ' (Romans 5:1). That must be the core of the special peace which Jesus alone can give. Scripture refers several times to the 'gospel of peace'. The good news is that Jesus' death gives us access to a peaceful relationship with God; beforehand, our sin had made that relationship impossible. This blood-bought, intimate relationship with the creator of the universe has to be the single most amazing, important and never-changing fact in our lives.

One of the best expositions of the gospel I have ever heard came from an agnostic, a lecturer in English literature, talking about Milton's epic poem *Samson Agonistes*. 'Although on one level the story of Samson ends in tragedy,' he said, 'in the deepest sense tragedy can't exist for a Christian. Death and destruction hurt grievously, but they don't lead to despair because God is ultimately in charge. Even if Christians go wrong as Samson did, God forgives and they spend a blissful eternity with him. And, as with Samson, often God redeems the situation in some way as well.'

Lord, I don't always feel peaceful on the surface, but thank you that deep down I know the most important thing in my life is that I have peace with you. I did nothing to earn that peace, so nothing can take it away! Help me to wear the shoes of the gospel of peace at all times, so that my whole life shows others how they can find this amazing peace with you too. Amen.

CL

Remembrance Sunday 8 November   John 15:13; 1 John 3:16 (NIV)

The death that made a difference

Greater love has no one than this, that he lay down his life for his friends.

This is how we know what love is: Jesus Christ laid down his life for us.

11 November 1918. Armistice Day. The end of a war that was expected to be 'the war to end all wars'. Remembrance Day was instituted to commemorate the millions who died in those four years. Millions more have died in other wars since, some as innocent victims and others because, freely or as conscripts, they have gone to fight and have laid down their lives for others. We honour them. Their deaths have been used to bring temporary peace. But, tragically, many of those deaths have made no major difference. They have not changed human hearts; they have not diminished the lust for power which is the basic cause of most wars.

Jesus' death was different. His love sent him voluntarily to his death on the cross. His death looked like a disaster but it ended in the triumph of his resurrection. And although he was put to death by wicked people, it was in God's purpose. For on the cross 'he himself bore our sins in his body on the tree, so that we might die to sins and live for righteousness' (1 Peter 2:24). His death can make a difference to each one of us. I used to look on his death as a mere matter of history. I did not doubt that he had died on a cross or that his resurrection had happened. But it all seemed fairly irrelevant to me in the twentieth century, until I recognized that my own character had similar elements to the people who were responsible for the wars. Then I saw that I needed Jesus for myself: his death meant that I could be forgiven; his resurrection meant that he was alive to be my living companion; and he wanted to give me the gift of his Spirit to live inside me and to change me.

We may not know, we cannot tell, what pains he had to bear;
But we believe it was for us he hung and suffered there.
C.F. Alexander

RG

MONDAY 9 NOVEMBER — *John 20:30–31 (NIV)*

Who is Jesus?

Jesus did many other miraculous signs in the presence of his disciples, which are not recorded in this book. But these are written that you may believe that Jesus is the Christ, the Son of God, and that by believing you may have life in his name.

At the end of his gospel, John, one of Jesus' special disciples, tells us why he wrote it. He wanted people to know who Jesus is and to experience new life through him. For the next two weeks we will read in this gospel how some of the people Jesus met came to believe in him.

The first person we meet is another John—John the Baptist. He was a striking figure, bold in his preaching, adamant that he was not the longed-for Messiah, but his forerunner. John was a mighty man and a humble one. 'I'm not even good enough to untie that one's shoelaces,' he said. He did not want to draw attention to himself; he wanted people to look at Jesus. Read John 1:29–34. We see him speaking about Jesus in three ways.

The Lamb of God. John baptized in water those who wanted to turn from their sin (Matthew 3:11), but he knew that baptism in water did not, by itself, wash away sin. The sacrificial lamb of the Old Testament was a symbol of God's forgiving, cleansing work in us ('a shadow of the good things that are coming' is how one New Testament writer puts it). John saw that Jesus was the real thing, the one who came to deal with the sin of the world.

He who will baptize with the Holy Spirit. The Holy Spirit is God's gift, through Jesus, of the life and power that enables us to change.

The Son of God. This was a bold statement for the Jews who believed strongly in only one God. God on earth in human form as well as God the holy one in heaven? It was unthinkable! But John wanted his readers to be clear from the beginning: Jesus is the Son of God.

Jesus, please show me who you are, that I may find life in your name.

RG

TUESDAY 10 NOVEMBER *John 1:35–42 (NIV)*

Found him!

Andrew, Simon Peter's brother, was one of the two who heard what John had said and who had followed Jesus. The first thing Andrew did was to find his brother Simon and tell him, 'We have found the Messiah' (that is, the Christ). And he brought him to Jesus.

John the Baptist did not want his disciples to cling to him. He wanted them to discover Jesus. Today's reading is a lovely example of the process of discovery that many people experience.

1. John 'the expert' pointed Jesus out to them: 'Look, the Lamb of God.' That was a big claim—the one who would be the ultimate sacrifice 'to take away the sins of the world' as we read yesterday. Andrew and his friend were intrigued and wanted to know more.

2. They took the next step and went to investigate. Jesus made it easy for them with a gentle question: 'What do you want?'

3. They were not yet sure about him; 'Teacher' was a safe way to address him. 'Where are you staying?' They seemed tentative, but they wanted to know more.

4. He gave them the invitation they hoped for, so they went to his home and stayed several hours. We don't know how their conversation went, but the encounter was enough to convince the two men that Jesus was the one predicted in the Old Testament who would come from God to rescue his people. 'We've found the Messiah!'

5. This was not the only 'finding' in the story. Andrew was so excited with his discovery of Jesus that he promptly went in search of his brother, to bring him in too. It is often the newest Christians who are the most eager to tell their friends about Jesus. Andrew is far less prominent among the disciples than Peter, but in John's Gospel we always see him introducing someone else to Jesus.

6. When Simon met Jesus, he found a person who had divine insight about who he was now and about the mature, reliable leader he would later become.

Where are you in your process of discovering Jesus?

RG

WEDNESDAY 11 NOVEMBER *John 1:43–49 (NIV)*

The divine X-ray

When Jesus saw Nathaniel approaching, he said of him, 'Here is a true Israelite, in whom there is nothing false.' 'How do you know me?' Nathaniel asked. Jesus answered, 'I saw you while you were still under the fig tree before Philip called you.' Then Nathaniel declared, 'Rabbi, you are the Son of God.'

There was a time in my Christian life when my spiritual well had run very dry. I was desperately empty but hoped to keep that hidden from other people. Yet I feared that some of the spiritually sensitive people around me could see past my defensive exterior to the hollowness inside. I was scared of God, too, afraid of how he viewed my barrenness. Mercifully, his love, expressed by those same people, melted my defences. Now I am glad to know that my heavenly Father sees right inside me. It is often said that 'he knows the worst about me, yet loves me just the same'.

Did Nathaniel feel rather like that? Jesus had made an immediate impact on Philip, who came, excitedly, to tell Nathaniel about Jesus. Nathaniel was scornful: 'Surely nothing good can come from Nazareth!' But he had a shock as he approached Jesus. This stranger seemed to know him. 'How do you know me?' 'I saw you,' said Jesus. It was not merely casual observation of a person sitting under a tree. 'I knew you. I understood you.' The divine X-ray eyes had been in operation.

The awareness of Jesus' perception moved Nathaniel from scepticism to belief: 'Teacher. Son of God. King of Israel.' It did not take him long to recognize who Jesus was. Then Jesus added the picture, strange at first sight, of heaven open and angels going up and down a stairway (implied from a reference to Jacob's dream in Genesis 28:12). The message is that through Jesus, who is both God and man, the way between heaven and earth is open, not just for the angels but for ordinary people who believe in him.

God knows you intimately. Does that make you want to come closer to him or to shrink back? 'Lord, please help me to feel safe with you, that I may find the way to heaven open for me.'

RG

THURSDAY 12 NOVEMBER   John 2:1–11 (NIV)

Transformation

Jesus said to the servants, 'Fill the jars with water'; so they filled them to the brim. Then he told them, 'Now draw some out and take it to the master of the banquet.'

My son was married on the afternoon of Princess Diana's funeral. The clergyman reminded us that Jesus was present both at the tomb of his friend Lazarus and also at this wedding in Cana. Jesus has shared the whole range of human emotions. He understands from the inside what we go through, as well as seeing us with his divine X-ray eyes.

But that is not the heart of this incident. It is a story about transformation. An embarrassing situation was turned around, so that those who were in the know saw more of Jesus' glory and power. The caterers had miscalculated. The wine was finished. We can imagine the panic behind the scenes! Mary became aware of the situation and approached Jesus—who seems to give her a brush-off. 'Dear woman, why do you involve me?' But she must have sensed greater openness than his recorded words imply. 'Do whatever he tells you,' she told the servants. She showed great trust in her son's willingness and ability to act. 'Fill the jars with water,' Jesus told them. They showed their obedience as they filled the jars to the brim—probably with water that was fit for washing but not for drinking. They showed even greater trust as they went to draw from the jars. There was nothing to show that Jesus had acted. Yet the wine they drew out was the very best provided at the feast.

But Jesus is not only able to change water into wine. He changes people. He takes ordinary people, impure people and transforms us inside. The difference is seen in our speech, our behaviour, our relationships. But our co-operation, our trust and obedience are as vital as that of Mary and the servants.

Let the beauty of Jesus be seen in me,
All his wondrous compassion and purity,
Oh thou Saviour divine, all my nature refine,
Till the beauty of Jesus be seen in me.
ALBERT OSBORN

RG

FRIDAY 13 NOVEMBER *John 3:1–15 (NIV)*

New birth, new life

Jesus declared, 'I tell you the truth, no one can see the kingdom of God unless he is born again.' 'How can a man be born when he is old?' Nicodemus asked.

Nicodemus was one of the élite, a member of the Sanhedrin, which, even under the Roman overlords, had wide powers of religious, civil and criminal jurisdiction. Other Pharisees were threatened and alarmed by Jesus. But Nicodemus was intrigued. He saw that here was no ordinary teacher, but he was not yet ready to step out of line publicly. So he slipped out in the dark to visit Jesus. An important conversation followed, recorded only in this gospel. Maybe John was the only disciple present. Nicodemus' opening words asked, in effect, 'Teacher, please tell me more about who you are.'

At first sight Jesus appears to ignore the unspoken question. Nicodemus is mystified: 'Born again? What are you talking about? We can't re-enter our mother's womb!' Jesus explains further: 'I'm not talking about physical birth. I'm talking about spiritual birth—my Spirit giving life to your spirit. What's more, you can't control it any more than you can control the way the wind blows.' Wind, breath, spirit; the Greek word is the same (*pneuma*—the word from which we get pneumatic tyre and pneumonia). Wind gives life to a dying fire; breath gives life to a baby; the Spirit gives life to a person's spirit. Jesus makes it clear that the new life from the Spirit is essential if we are to belong in God's kingdom.

'And that,' Jesus told Nicodemus, 'is for you down on earth. If you cannot grasp this, you will not be able to understand anything about heaven. You said I'm a teacher come from God. Yes, indeed I am. And you, Nicodemus, know the story about the bronze snake Moses made, through which the dying Israelites were healed. I'm like that snake. Through me, and through my Spirit, you can find that new life, eternal life.'

Lord, I do not really understand, but I want this new life.

RG

Saturday 14 November   John 4:4–15(NIV)

Living water

Jesus answered her, 'If you knew the gift of God and who it is that asks you for a drink, you would have asked him and he would have given you living water.'

This is a story of surprises. For a start, the disciples were surprised at their route north. Normally the Jews preferred to use a longer, roundabout way between Jerusalem and Galilee in order to avoid the hated Assyrian Jews who lived in Samaria. So the woman who came to the well was surprised to see a Jew in her town. Nor did she expect to find anyone at the well in the noonday heat ('the sixth hour'). She went then to avoid the snubs of the 'respectable' people who drew their water in the cool of dawn or dusk.

Yet another surprise followed. This man actually spoke to her. He asked for a drink. It was not, of course, merely a request from a thirsty man, but a way to start a conversation. For tired though he was, Jesus needed to meet this woman; that was why he 'had' to go through Samaria. Having asked for water from the well, he moved quickly to arouse her curiosity further: 'I can give you living water.' Her mind was set on practicalities: 'But you've not got a bucket. Even our forefather Jacob couldn't manage without one. How can you?

Then Jesus told her more. 'All who drink this water will be thirsty again, but those who drink the water I give them will never thirst. Indeed, the water I give them will become in them a spring of water welling up to eternal life.' Water welling up to eternal life—that sounded good, even though she still thought of it as a short-cut to avoid coming to the well for her H_2O. 'Give me this water.'

There are times in our lives when we know we are empty, dry, dissatisfied. We can turn to the one who quenches that sort of thirst and gives us eternal life. 'Jesus, please give me your living water.'

RG

Sunday 15 November
John 4:16–26 (NIV)

Towards the truth

A time is coming and has now come when the true worshippers will worship the Father in spirit and in truth, for they are the kind of worshippers the Father seeks. God is spirit, and his worshippers must worship in spirit and in truth.

Surprise was followed by shock. As Jesus led the woman forward on her journey of faith, he needed to confront her lifestyle and to show her that she couldn't pull any wool over his eyes. 'Bring your husband.' 'I haven't got one.' 'I know. You've had five and you're not married to the man you're with now.' His inside knowledge startled her. This was getting too near the bone. Her sin had been exposed and she felt vulnerable. So she tried to side-step to a 'religious' discussion. That rings true! We do not enjoy being faced with uncomfortable home truths. Better to change the topic of conversation.

'Tell me, sir. You've got insight from God. You'll be able to answer the disputed question about the right place to worship. Up there [pointing to nearby Mount Gerizim, where the Samaritans held their religious festivals], or in Jerusalem?' But Jesus was not interested in the place of worship; her question was not relevant. Yes, the Samaritans used only the Pentateuch (the first five books of the Bible) rather than the whole Old Testament. So their understanding of God was less than that of the Jews, through whose race, in Jesus himself, salvation would come. But a new era had dawned. God would be worshipped in spirit and truth. In spirit, not tied down to any one place. In truth, because of truth revealed in Jesus Christ.

The woman was still puzzled. Maybe she hoped to defer any decision and to evade this man who knew so much but talked to her out of her depth. 'When Messiah comes, he'll explain it all'—later. 'I am that Messiah,' said Jesus. Not later, but now.

Does the woman's attitude ring bells for you? Intrigued about Jesus but unwilling to face home truths; ready to discuss abstract issues but wanting to put off difficult decisions? He faces us with himself: 'I am he.'

RG

MONDAY 16 NOVEMBER *John 4:27–42 (NIV)*

The early crop

Leaving her water jar, the woman went back to the town and said to the people, 'Come, see a man who told me everything I ever did. Could this be the Christ?' They came out of the town and made their way towards him.

This has been a story of surprises. The disciples, after their trip to the town to buy food, were in for another shock. They returned to find Jesus talking with a woman—what's more, a Samaritan woman. And why did she need to come for water in the heat of the day? Their eyebrows were raised, but none of them dared question him. Instead they urged him to eat something, but their comments show that their minds were as earthbound as the woman's had been.

We might at first think that today's reading has two independent strands: Jesus talking with his disciples about harvest, and the woman bringing some other residents of the town to meet him. But the harvest of which Jesus spoke was not the harvest of wheat. It is the harvest of people in God's kingdom, brought about by those who, like Jesus, are intent on serving God in whatever capacity he wants (as 'sower', 'reaper' or the person who tends the growing crop). 'My food is to do the will of him who sent me and to finish his work' was Jesus' motto for life. Could we adopt it as our own?

Here, in Samaria of all surprising places, are the first fruits of the harvest. The woman, almost persuaded that Jesus was the Messiah, went to share the news in the town. The disciples had returned with food. She returned with people. When they listened to Jesus themselves they decided that here was the one who was not merely the Messiah for the Jews but the Saviour of the world.

Earlier Jesus talked with Nicodemus—a man of the privileged Jewish ruling class. Now we see him with a despised Samaritan woman. He is no differentiator of people.

RG

TUESDAY 17 NOVEMBER John 4:43–54 (NIV)

Healed from afar

The royal official said, 'Sir, come down before my child dies.'
Jesus replied, 'You may go. Your son will live.'

A member of the Sanhedrin; a Samaritan woman; now it was a royal official who turned to Jesus for help. He travelled several hours to find him, to beg him to come to his dying son. As at the wedding, Jesus' first reply sounds hard: 'You don't believe without miracles.' But the man was not deterred. He stuck, single-mindedly, to his request: 'Come down before my child dies.' His faith had been tested. Now it was both rewarded—and tested further.

He left with Jesus' promise—but he still had many hours to travel before he had news. But 'he took Jesus at his word'. I like that. He trusted—and even before he got home after his overnight journey, his servants met him with the news of his son's recovery. His faith had already been rewarded. It was strengthened further when he heard that the boy's temperature had dropped at the exact time that Jesus had spoken to him.

Jesus still heals today, though not always in the way we hope. This story reminded me of an answer to a simple prayer for healing that led to a renewal of faith. A cousin, a very occasional churchgoer, phoned from 200 miles away to tell us of her husband's serious illness in hospital. She asked tentatively, 'Please think of him at bedtime.' 'Yes, certainly we'll pray for him then. Would you like me to pray now, on the phone?' I can't remember how I prayed, but next evening she phoned again. She had seen his temperature drop dramatically during the night; she asked me to pray to give thanks. Her next call, a few days later, gave us the progress report—and she prayed, aloud, on the phone. Thereafter, that couple were stuck into their local church. Their faith was fanned into life as they saw God at work in the husband's recovery.

We never know how God will answer prayer for healing. We need to trust that he really does know best.

RG

WEDNESDAY 18 NOVEMBER   *John 5:1–9, 14 (NIV)*

Do you want to be healed?

When Jesus saw him lying there and learned that he had been in this condition for a long time, he asked him, 'Do you want to get well?'

Jesus' question was a penetrating one. We might think, 'The man had been ill for thirty-eight years; of course he wanted to get well!' But it is easy to get so used to being helpless that we are reluctant to exchange dependence for responsibility. 'There's no one to help me.' A lame excuse or a genuine reason? Jesus, who always knew what was going on inside a person, saw it as a reason. 'Get up!' Immediately the man obeyed, and found he was healed. Later Jesus met him again and warned him that, although he was physically well again, he needed to change inside as well. Jesus is interested in the whole person—body, mind and spirit. He wants to see wholeness in us.

I was excited to hear recently from a physiotherapist friend about a West Indian Christian who, when visiting his wife in hospital, started to talk about Jesus to the woman in the next bed whose legs were paralysed. After a time she came to believe in Jesus and wanted to be baptized. My friend drove her to the local church and wheeled her in. After her baptism she was given Communion; she was so weak they had to lift her hands to eat the bread. As this was done, she said 'I'm healed. I want to stand up!' They remonstrated. Then she said, 'I can feel my legs!' So she stood up. And back in hospital, she *walked* into the ward. God healed her physically and helped her to put her life straight as well as bringing her to real trust in him.

Can God do it? Do you want it? Will you let him? Those are three questions I often ask people who are looking for change in their lives. The answer does not have to be a confident 100 per cent 'yes' to each question. 'I suppose you can do it—and yes, I want it enough to let you work in whatever way you know is best' gives God the green light to act.

RG

THURSDAY 19 NOVEMBER *John 8:1–11 (NIV)**

Free for change

Jesus straightened up and asked her, 'Woman, where are they? Has no one condemned you?' 'No one, sir,' she said. 'Then neither do I condemn you,' Jesus declared. 'Go now and leave your life of sin.'

It looks like a chauvinistic scene! The woman had been caught red-handed in adultery. Why had they let the man go and only brought the woman to Jesus? The Pharisees primarily wanted to trap Jesus into contradicting the Law of Moses, but they preferred to bring shame on the woman rather than the man involved. Their plans went wrong! The accusation against her rebounded. They slunk away, with their own guilt exposed, while the woman had a new start in life. And for Jesus? As in all his encounters with the Jews, his divine wisdom stands out supreme. There was no way they could point a finger at him.

The woman knew she was guilty. Jesus knew she was guilty, and he did not condemn her sin. He forgave her. She no longer needed to carry the burden of her guilt. But he expected her to change: 'Go now and leave your life of sin.' Forgiveness should go hand in hand with repentance. Our forgiveness was not bought cheaply: Jesus paid with his own life. We do not have to earn our freedom, but we thank him by turning away from the sin, to live as new people. I believe the woman went away with a clear conscience and a thankful heart, to make a new start.

Most of us know what it is like to wait for our luggage by an airport carousel. Imagine that each of those suitcases holds a load of guilt. Each of us must claim our own luggage. But then we do not stagger away carrying it. We put it straight on the trolley. The 'guilt' trolley is marked with a cross, and Jesus is the porter.

---

* Modern scholars agree that this story was not in John's original manuscript. But they also believe that it is a true story about Jesus that was passed on verbally. The second-century Christians were anxious to retain it in written form.

RG

FRIDAY 20 NOVEMBER   *John 11:17–27 (NIV)*

Faith meets doubt

'Lord,' Martha said to Jesus, 'if you had been here, my brother would not have died. But I know that even now God will give you whatever you ask.' Jesus said to her, 'Your brother will rise again.'

Jesus had often stayed in Bethany in the home of Lazarus and his two sisters. Now he had come after receiving a message that Lazarus was seriously ill. He had not hurried. He had even waited for two days before setting out. He was confident that this was a time for God's power and glory to be seen through Lazarus being raised from death. When he arrived Lazarus had already been in the grave for four days. Martha the activist went to meet him, while her quieter, more contemplative sister stayed at home.

Martha was free enough with Jesus to rebuke him for his delay. 'If you had been here…' It is good for us to be honest with God about how we feel. It is all right, even, for us to tell him if we feel he has let us down—so long as we don't get stuck there. Martha moved on: 'But I know that even now God will give you whatever you ask.' She trusted Jesus, although she was not sure what she could hope for. God understands the fear and the faith that often exist side by side within us. Suppose I have a glass containing water halfway up. 'It's half full.' 'It's half empty.' Apparently contradictory statements—but both are true! Our 'faith glass' can be half empty (with doubt) and half full (with faith) at the same time. God wants us to be wholly honest with him, but not to allow our trust to be wholly submerged by our doubt or our anger.

This honesty was an important prelude to the conversation that developed; we will think more about that tomorrow. It led to Martha's clear affirmation of her faith in Jesus: 'I believe that you are the Christ, the Son of God, who was to come into the world.'

'I do believe; help me overcome my unbelief!' (Mark 9:24)

                                                                    RG

SATURDAY 21 NOVEMBER   John 11:25–44 (NIV)

Resurrection life

Jesus said to her, 'I am the resurrection and the life. He who believes in me will live, even though he dies; and whoever lives and believes in me will never die. Do you believe this?'

When Mary came to meet Jesus her cry was the same as her sister's: 'If only you had been here!' Others who saw Jesus in tears with the sisters commented, 'Surely he could have prevented this death.' Yes, he could. But they already had evidence of his power to heal. Now even greater power was to be seen: 'Lazarus, come out!' We can imagine the tension outside the tomb. They waited. Then the man who had been in the grave for four days, whose body should have been beginning to putrefy, walked out.

Martha, Mary and their friends must have rejoiced to have Lazarus restored to them. Tears were turned to joy. But what of Jesus' tears earlier? They were not the tears of the bereaved, for he knew what his Father was going to do. Were they tears of compassion for the grief of his friends? Perhaps. But they were more. They were tears of one who came to earth to identify with the pain and sin of the world. He knew he faced a horrific death with the agony of crucifixion and the even greater agony of being separated from his Father as he carried the load of the world's sin.

Jesus, however, could see beyond the grave: 'I am the resurrection and the life.' Not only his own resurrection on the first Easter Sunday. Not only Lazarus' emergence from the grave, a miracle in itself. Jesus was speaking of something else. The believer, he says, will die physically. But the new life he gives us goes beyond the grave, to eternity. 'Eternal life' is a quality of life that starts on this earth. 'Whoever lives and believes in me will never die.' But 'even though they die [physically] those who believe in me will live (spiritually) now and to eternity.'

Jesus asks us the same question he asked Martha: 'Do you believe this?'
RG

Sunday 22 November   Isaiah 55:12–13 (NIV)

Joy in freedom

You will go out in joy and be led forth in peace; the mountains and hills will burst into song before you, and all the trees of the field will clap their hands. Instead of the thornbush will grow the pine tree, and instead of briers the myrtle will grow.

This verse is all about freedom—of going on to a new life from the old—away from what was an unhappy experience into a new happiness. Here, through the words of Isaiah, God promises his children that they will leave the land of Babylon, where they had been living in exile—that they will go out in joy and peace (not in fear for their lives). And as they looked at the mountains and the hills and the trees it was as if all of creation was rejoicing with them as they walked into freedom.

Living in exile is the everyday experience of many in this twentieth century, just as it was in the days of Isaiah. Refugees live away from their own lands because of wars and famine, political differences and racial hatred. Every day in this country alone many arrive on the Channel ferries from the Continent seeking asylum—looking for freedom, looking for a new and better life. When we read the papers or watch the news on television we are reminded of those who live in exile.

Our own cities and neighbourhoods are full of people who live every day without this joy and peace. So what Isaiah was saying to God's children so long ago is also written for God's children of today. These verses are speaking of a personal transformation from being in captivity to sin and of being called into a new life in Christ. With this transformation we experience a joy and peace that has nothing to do with our personal circumstances, but everything to do with our relationship with the Creator. And when our relationship with God is right, then the thornbushes and briers in life will be changed to the pine and the myrtle—plants that stay green all year round!

MR

MONDAY 23 NOVEMBER — Proverbs 15:30 (NIV)

A joyful heart

A cheerful look brings joy to the heart, and good news gives health to the bones.

Whenever I look up a verse in the book of Proverbs I end up reading on and on, forgetting what I was originally looking for! It is full of wise sayings, mostly attributed to Solomon and a circle of wise men, to give practical advice on the art of living. This chapter is full of gems: 'A gentle answer turns away wrath, but a harsh word stirs up anger' (v. 1); 'Better a little with the fear of the Lord than great wealth with turmoil' (v. 16); 'Better a meal with vegetables where there is love than a fattened calf with hatred' (v. 17). Here I am, digressing again! The verse I was originally looking up is verse 30. A cheerful look—a happy face—does indeed give joy, not only to the person who is smiling but to everyone else on the receiving end of that smile.

When we had just moved to a new parish I was anxious not to cause offence by walking past someone I should recognize, so I developed the habit of smiling at absolutely everyone. I got some rather startled looks from total strangers—but I also got many more smiles in return (also from some total strangers!) It does us all good to see people smiling. A smile can be quite contagious, especially on a rainy November day! It is interesting that the first thing most children draw is a round face with a big smile—for the mother's smile is the first thing a tiny baby can see. If its mother is smiling then all is well in the world for that tiny, helpless being. Maybe this is why we feel secure, as adults, when we are greeted with a smile.

The cheerful look brings joy to the heart, yet earlier in this chapter, in verse 13, we read, 'A happy heart makes the face cheerful.' Our faces reflect how we feel inside, and when we show that happiness we have even more joy to share.

Make sure you smile today, no matter what the day has in store for you, and take time to pray for anyone you know who seems sad.

MR

TUESDAY 24 NOVEMBER　　　　　　　　　*Isaiah 9:2–3 (GNB)*

God-given joy

The people who walked in darkness have seen a great light. They lived in a land of shadows, but now light is shining on them. You have given them great joy, Lord; you have made them happy.

Complete darkness in the middle of the day is a weather phenomenon that doesn't often happen, but when it does it is quite alarming. This happened once when we were driving home from our summer holiday in Norfolk. We set off mid-afternoon when the clouds were beginning to gather, the sky became increasingly dark and threatening the further we travelled south, until eventually we were in the middle of a violent thunderstorm. Pitch darkness seemed to enclose our whole world as we crawled along in appalling conditions, our headlights only lighting up the rain! And then we saw, on the horizon, a brilliant strip of bright turquoise sky. The contrast between the darkness and the light was dramatic. And when we eventually came out into a brilliant, sunny afternoon we got out of the car just to enjoy the beauty all around us.

The people of Israel had been 'walking in darkness'. They had been under threat from a powerful neighbour, Assyria, and they had lost their trust in God and were living in sin and disobedience. They had no hope—either in their own ability to keep out of trouble, or in God who had been their strength in the past. They were living in a land of shadows. 'But now,' writes the prophet, 'light is shining on them. You have given them great joy.' In verse 6 he gives the reason for their joy: 'For to us a child is born, to us a son is given… he will be called Wonderful Counsellor, Mighty God, Everlasting Father, Prince of Peace.' The light that was to come after the darkness was the promised Messiah, Jesus, the light of the world.

Illness, bereavement, depression can give us times of living in the shadows. But the light and love of Jesus will eventually break through the darkness and give a renewed joy in living in his glorious light.

Read Isaiah 9:1–7.

MR

WEDNESDAY 25 NOVEMBER *Romans 15:13 (GNB)*

Inner joy

May God, the source of hope, fill you with all joy and peace by means of your faith in him, so that your hope will continue to grow by the power of the Holy Spirit.

My husband's favourite aunt, a wonderful person now well into her nineties, has a fund of amusing stories about her childhood. Apparently her mother always twisted her mouth into a terrible grimace whenever she looked in the mirror to adjust her hat or tidy her hair. Mirrors could make you vain, the small girl was told. So to make sure you weren't tempted to be proud of your appearance you scowled into the mirror! That seems a strange way to try to influence your inner self.

When you looked in the mirror this morning, what did you see? A face that is not as beautiful or as young as you would like it to be? Is it the face of someone who is not looking forward to going to work today—or is the sun shining, even in November, and life seems very good at the moment? How much do our faces reflect our inner selves? In this one verse from Romans, Paul writes of hope, joy and peace—all qualities that are God-given and have nothing to do with outward circumstances. God-given joy and peace are within us and come from the certainty and confidence that we can never be separated from the love of God. We may be trying to deal with what seems a hopeless situation with someone we love (or find difficult to love), but no situation is hopeless when we know we have the power of God as a resource. As this verse says, 'your hope will continue to grow by the power of the Holy Spirit.'

So be reassured by today's verse. The face you see in the mirror is loved by God, and the person you see reflected there is full of joy and peace.

Fill Thou my life, O Lord my God,
in ev'ry part with praise,
that my whole being may proclaim
Thy being and Thy ways.
H. BONAR (1808–89)

MR

THURSDAY 26 NOVEMBER   *Philemon 7 (GNB)*

Joy in relationships

Your love, dear brother, has brought me great joy and much encouragement! You have cheered the hearts of all of God's people.

Paul was in prison in Rome and Philemon was a church leader in Colossae. They had probably never met, yet all that Paul had heard had given him much joy and encouragement. Clearly Philemon was a truly godly man as he had 'cheered the hearts of all God's people'. To Paul he was 'a dear brother'. All those who were Christians were part of one ever-growing family.

Onesimus, Philemon's runaway slave, had met Paul in Rome and had become a believer so he was now part of the family of God, even though he was still officially a runaway slave and liable to be punished by death. Paul appealed to Philemon to treat Onesimus as 'a dear brother in Christ'. He points out how much better he will be as a Christian slave! As this letter is included in our New Testament, I assume that he was indeed welcomed back as a brother.

The joy that the early Christians experienced, and the sense of being part of one great family, is something I discovered many years ago. I emigrated to Canada when I was twenty-one. Everything was one great adventure—until I stood on the deck of the ship and waved goodbye to the shores of England. I was leaving my family, my friends and everything that was familiar. Suddenly I felt quite desolate and alone and very miserable. At dinner that night I found myself sharing a table with a young Canadian couple, and within five minutes I had discovered that they too were Christians, that the husband was on the staff of Wycliffe Bible College in Toronto and one of his students was a friend of mine from my church youth group in England. It was wonderful; I felt I had known them for years by the time we had finished that meal. We were in the same family—brothers and sisters in Christ.

Read Paul's letter to Philemon.

                                                               MR

Friday 27 November   *John 16:22 (NIV)*

Sorrow to joy

Now is your time of grief, but I will see you again and you will rejoice, and no one will take away your joy.

Jesus knew that he was about to be taken prisoner and killed, and he knew that his disciples would be devastated. So he was trying to prepare them for what was to be a very difficult time for everyone. He told them that the bad times wouldn't be for ever, that they would see him again and they would experience a happiness and joy that could never be taken away from them.

Yet I don't really think that the disciples understood what he was saying. Just like us, really. We may listen to what others say about various aspects of life, but it is not until you experience difficulties yourself that you know what it feels like. The example that Jesus gave to his friends (mostly men!) was of childbirth—just as any suffering for a woman is forgotten in the joy of holding her newborn child, so the disciples' grief would turn to joy when they met Jesus again.

This verse also says something to us about life in the here and now. Living as a Christian can at times be quite uncomfortable, as if we are trying to swim against the tide of the way 'everybody lives these days'. It sometimes looks as if those all around us are having a wonderful life: high salaries, huge houses, expensive clothes, overseas holidays and lots of fun! But the joy that comes from success, fame and money will not last. People who spend a lifetime looking for happiness through possessions usually end up disappointed, and even those who depend on other people for happiness will in the end be parted by death. The world cannot offer everlasting joy. The joy that Christ gives us is part of us now, it always will be part of us and no one can take it away.

Read John 16:17–33 and first look at what Jesus was saying to the disciples. Then read it again to see what it is saying to us today.

MR

SATURDAY 28 NOVEMBER   John 16:24 (NIV)

Complete joy

Until now you have not asked for anything in my name. Ask and you will receive, and your joy will be complete.

I can't ever remember being told, as a child, that it was rude to ask for presents. Maybe, because my childhood years were also the war years, there wasn't much point in asking for toys or books or clothes because such luxuries were just not available. Whatever the reason, I have always found it difficult to ask for anything I really wanted. I just hope that somehow those nearest and dearest to me will be able to read my mind. Sometimes that happens, but mostly it doesn't and I have no one to blame but myself!

However, surely God knows everything about us. He knows what we are thinking and feeling. He knows what we need—so why do we have to ask him? Yet here Jesus is clearly telling us to 'ask'. Quite early in Jesus' ministry, when crowds were following him everywhere, he went up a hill and sat down and began to teach. And one of the things he said then was that we had to ask: 'Ask and it will be given to you … Which of you, if his son asks for bread, will give him a stone? Or if he asks for a fish, will give him a snake? If you, then … know how to give good gifts to your children, how much more will your Father in heaven give good gifts to those who ask him' (Matthew 7:7, 9–11).

The verse that we are thinking about today is something Jesus said right at the end of his earthly ministry, just before his arrest and crucifixion. Up to this point his disciples would, like all good Jews, have prayed directly to God. But they had a new relationship with God, made possible by Jesus. We can ask our heavenly Father for anything because of Jesus, and it is through Jesus that our prayers are answered and we are blessed. 'Ask and you will receive, and your joy will be complete.'

God knows your greatest need, so pray to him about it; he will listen, and your joy will be full.

MR

SUNDAY 29 NOVEMBER / Romans 12:1 (LB)

Jesus look-alikes

I plead with you to give your bodies to God. Let them be a living sacrifice, holy—the kind he can accept. When you think of what he has done for you, is this too much to ask?

'Who does he "take after"?' That's what we usually ask when a baby arrives, and if we want to please the proud father we'll say 'it' looks like him! Paul tells us twice that God hopes we'll all 'take after' Jesus as we grow up as Christians (2 Corinthians 3:18; Romans 8:29). He wants us to be Jesus look-alikes in every situation, in the way we think, speak, act and relate to others. 'Some hope,' we might think, 'in our materialistic, pleasure-loving age!' Yet when Paul was writing to a group of new Christians in a remarkably similar cultural setting, he gave them some practical tips which we might well find helpful. Over the next two weeks we'll be looking at them in detail, but today Paul starts by telling us that the process of becoming like Jesus will cost us everything. We need to give our bodies to God as a living present—and our personalities, desires, dreams, feelings, thoughts, time, activities—everything! Jesus did that for us when he stepped down into our world, so to become like him we start by doing exactly the same.

When I was a child my favourite day-dream was imagining myself as a brave and noble missionary, dying a martyr's death in a jungle. I've since realized that it is a lot easier to die for God on one dramatic occasion than it is to live for him through the ordinary little hassles of every day. Jesus spent thirty out of his thirty-three years doing unimportant, boring little jobs in a small family business—but he did every single one of them for God.

Father God, I do want to be like Jesus but, when I look at the mess that's me, the idea seems utterly ridiculous. Please take every cell of my body and every detail of my life so you can start the job of moulding me into his image. Amen.

JRL

MONDAY 30 NOVEMBER   *Romans 12:2 (LB)*

Thinking like Jesus

Don't copy the behaviour and customs of this world, but be a new and different person with a fresh newness in all you do and think. Then you will learn from your own experience how his ways will really satisfy you.

It is one thing to give our bodies to God as a present, but of course we also have to give our minds. Most of us don't realize how easily we are influenced by this world's thinking patterns. A friend of mine watched TV for a whole evening and told me she'd counted eighty-eight occasions when she had seen God's rules or principles for our behaviour flouted or broken.

It's not just the media who are to blame. We 'catch' our culture's value systems and coping strategies from our families in early childhood, and our friends and workmates, as we grow up. We absorb popular catchphrases which are totally contrary to God's way of thinking—statements like, 'Oh it's OK, *everybody* does it', or 'You must look after number one', or 'I've got a right to be happy.' When we finally hand over our minds to God they are so cluttered up by this kind of stuff that it seems to take him a lifetime to alter our thought patterns. Perhaps his job could be speeded dramatically if we spent as much time absorbing Jesus through the Bible and Christian books as we spend absorbing the world through videos and the telly!

My mind is always slipping into 'worry mode', but one of my favourite verses is Isaiah 26:3: 'You will keep in perfect peace him whose mind is steadfast, because he trusts in you' (NIV). When I start panicking it is usually because I'm concentrating on all my problems and letting them dominate my thinking. If I can mentally turn away from them and concentrate on the Lord, and all the promises he has made to me, I soon get my peace back again.

Lord, my brain buzzes with so many negative thoughts I feel sick of living with myself sometimes! Please help me think about life, myself and other people the way you do. Amen.

JRL

TUESDAY 1 DECEMBER   *Romans 12:3, 10, 16 (LB)*
Acting like Jesus

Be honest in your estimate of yourselves, measuring your value by how much faith God has given you. Love each other with brotherly affection and take delight in honouring each other. Work happily together. Don't try to act big. Don't try to get into the good books of important people, but enjoy the company of ordinary folks. And don't think you know it all!

Today Paul describes the kind of attitude towards others that we need if we want to be like Jesus. I guess he would heartily approve of the preacher who, looking sadly at a drunk in a gutter said softly, 'There but for the grace of God go I.'

We ask God to change us, but when he does we take the credit and start feeling so pleased with ourselves we look down on everyone else. You only have to listen to a few after-church conversations to realize how prone we all are to pride—the worst sin of all! Have you heard this kind of thing? 'Don't ask her to help, she's only a new Christian, she hasn't a clue!' 'My husband isn't nearly as far on as I am.' 'Oh, she's the sort who lurches from one problem to another!' 'I can't stand happy-clappies!' If we treat one another like that, no wonder non-churchgoers label us as judgmental.

Jesus had a lovely way of making everyone he met feel they really mattered to him. One day a half-naked woman was dragged to him by a crowd of respectable citizens. She had been caught in bed with someone else's husband and they were out for her blood. Instead of despising her, like everyone else, Jesus looked at her with such uncondemning love she was completely changed. His attitude gave her the confidence to start a new life (John 8:2–11). People can be crushed by our disapproval or set free by our encouragement.

When you think about other people, would you say you were more likely to look up at them in admiration for their good qualities, or down on them for their failures and mistakes?

JRL

WEDNESDAY 2 DECEMBER *Romans 12:4–5 (LB)*

Relating like Jesus

Just as there are many parts to our bodies, so it is with Christ's body. We are all parts of it, and it takes every one of us to make it complete, for we each have different work to do. So we belong to each other and each needs all the others.

I was hanging around London, killing time before an important interview. Feeling scared and lonely I went to a kiosk for a hot drink. I'll never forget the face of the lady who served me: her smile was so radiant that her black face positively shone. Without thinking I said, 'You must be a Christian!' 'I sure am!' she replied, and the moment she gripped my hand I stopped feeling alone or afraid. After chatting for five minutes we felt we'd known each other for ever!

Paul tells us today that the bond between Christians is closer than family; we are part of the living, moving, hearing, speaking, loving body of Jesus here on earth. A body so vast that it stretches right over the globe, yet linked together by a network of invisible 'veins and arteries'. Paul was so pleased with this 'body' idea that he expanded it when he wrote to a church in Corinth (1 Corinthians 12:12–31). We don't know how the Roman Christians were relating to each other, but in Corinth they were fighting like dogs and breaking Paul's heart. God wants us to be as close to each other as two toes on a foot, yet it seems as if we Christians are always quarrelling. We form ourselves into a lot of small, mutually exclusive groups, declaring we are the only ones who've 'got it right'.

We can't mend the broken body of Christ worldwide, but we are responsible for our own broken relationships. Has someone upset you? Jesus deliberately sat next to Judas Iscariot at the last supper and went out of his way to show him special kindness and courtesy. Could you treat your 'enemy' like that?

Could you write a list of the people you find difficult, and ask the Lord to help you treat them as Jesus would?

JRL

THURSDAY 3 DECEMBER Romans 12:6–7 (LB)

Serving like Jesus

God has given each of us the ability to do certain things well. So if God has given you the ability to prophesy, then prophesy whenever you can—as often as your faith is strong enough to receive a message from God. If your gift is that of serving others, serve them well. If you are a teacher, do a good job of teaching. If you are a preacher, see to it that your sermons are encouraging and helpful.

Peggy sat in church feeling utterly miserable. 'We all have a gift we can use to serve God,' said the voice from the pulpit. 'Except me,' thought Peggy. Everyone else in church seemed so talented but, since her children had left home and her husband had died, she felt so useless and too shy to get involved with church activities.

'We'll spend a moment in silence,' concluded the vicar, 'so everyone can ask God what is their spiritual gift.'

'There!' thought Peggy at the end of the prayer. 'That proves God never speaks to me.' The only word that had come into her head was 'soup'! On the way out of church the vicar said, 'Peggy, some of us take food to the homeless in London on Saturday nights. Could you make some soup next week?' It wasn't long before Peggy was not only making soup *each* week, but going with the team to ladle it out. As her confidence has grown she's made some special friendships with her 'regulars' and recently she told me, 'What they need, even more than hot soup, is someone who's got time to listen to them.'

So often we think it's the 'up-front' people who are important in our church communities. Today, however, Paul gives the private unseen gifts, like serving others, equal status with the public gifts of prophesy, preaching or teaching. A body needs hands and ears just as much as it needs a mouth!

Lord, I don't have much in the way of time or natural talents to give you, but, like the little boy who gave you his picnic lunch, please take what I have and use it to help others. Amen.

JRL

Friday 4 December   Romans 12:8b and 13 (LB)

Giving like Jesus

If God has given you money, be generous in helping others with it ... Those who offer comfort to the sorrowing should do so with Christian cheer. When God's children are in need, you be the one to help them out. And get into the habit of inviting guests home for dinner or if they need lodging, for the night.

That advice is all very well, if our families share our Christian commitment, but taking it too enthusiastically nearly finished Jemma's marriage. She discovered her gift was caring for people in trouble. She was an excellent listener and very generous with her time, energy and resources. Then one day her husband erupted. 'I work my guts out for this family, but when I come home tired, there's always some lame-dog here telling you a sob story. Supper's never ready because you've been out hospital visiting, and you keep giving my hard-earned money to a load of spongers!'

'Surely God wants me to help people?' Jemma asked her friend.

'Of course he does,' she replied, 'but perhaps your priorities are in the wrong order. Your personal relationship of love and friendship with God himself always comes first. Then your family and after that the things you do for God. You've been so busy working *for* him that you haven't had enough time to spend *with* him, and your family feels they come last for you nowadays. No wonder Tom's stroppy!'

Juggling priorities is always difficult. Some people so enjoy worship and being with God they don't notice the sad, lonely people in the world around them. Others are so absorbed by husband, children and job, God gets lost under the smart new furniture. Jesus gave all his time and energy to other people, but for the first thirty years of his life he gave everything he had to his family; it was only when they didn't need him so much that he was able to give himself to others.

Lord, the demands of other people pull me in all directions. Please keep on filling me up with yourself, because on my own I've got nothing left to give. Amen.

JRL

SATURDAY 5 DECEMBER · Romans 12:8 (NIV)

Leading like Jesus

If a man's gift… is leadership, let him govern diligently.

Before we all start bristling at the way Paul links the word 'leadership' with the word 'man', let me say that being a Christian leader isn't only about wearing your collar the wrong way round. It applies to anyone who influences others, i.e. helping with an Alpha group, Sunday school class, college or school Christian Union or ladies' meeting, or being a mother or child-minder.

The job of making God real to others is a serious one. Hebrews 13:17 says leaders will have to give an account of their work before God's throne one day. As we've already seen this week, it's no good saying, 'But I'm only there to make the tea (or soup).' In God's eyes our gifts are all equally important, so we are all equally responsible for the people we serve, whether that's thousands or just one. Jesus was the greatest leader of men ever, but he spent lots of his time with just three of his followers.

His leadership assignment was to show a group of people what God was really like and prepare them to go and share that information with the world. If you are a mother, or help run any kind of church activity, that is your commission too.

It wasn't so much what Jesus said about God which influenced his group, but the way he modelled God's love to them in the little practical details of life. Few of us realize how intently we are being watched by others all the time, and our children are the most critical observers of all. My mother never told me how vital it is to spend time alone with God each day, but every morning, however early I toddled into her bedroom, she was always reading her Bible. I don't remember anything my Sunday school teacher said, but I'll never forget how incredibly kind he was to me when my dog died.

Lord, help me to model your love to the people who 'watch' me today. Amen.

JRL

Sunday 6 December · Romans 12:9 (LB)

Loving like Jesus

Don't just pretend that you love others: really love them. Hate what is wrong. Stand on the side of the good.

I often struggle with how to act towards people I don't love—or even like! Selwyn Hughes once said, 'You can't always feel your way into actions but you can always act your way into feelings.' I find that statement most helpful, yet it seems to contradict what Paul is saying. Surely acting is pretending? Just a week after she became a Christian, Janet joined a little nurture group I once helped to run. She had never read the Bible before, but was determined to obey it to the letter. When we were talking about the knotty question of love, she suddenly looked very worried.

'But I could *never* love the woman who stole my Dad from Mum. She ruined my childhood. I won't even speak to her.' We calmed her down, saying that God never asks us to do anything without offering to help.

Then, a few days later, Janet rang me. 'My Dad's just phoned out of the blue,' she said tearfully. 'He's in the district and wants to pop in. He asked if he could bring Velma with him. I *do* want to love her, but how can I?' I told her to ask God to put *his* love in her heart. 'Then, even if you don't feel any love of your own, you will be able to love her with God's love. Just act out his love to her.'

'That's hypocrisy,' she protested.

'But you won't be insincere,' I replied. 'You actually will have love in your heart for Velma—not yours but God's. Just treat her as Jesus would.' Very doubtfully Janet agreed. Three hours later she burst through my front door, looking radiant.

'It worked!' she said. 'At first it felt very odd, fussing around her, chatting and smiling, but before they left I caught myself thinking how nice she is. Acting loving really did make me feel loving—well, a bit anyway, but it's a start isn't it?'

Lord, please fill my heart with your love towards… Amen.

JRL

MONDAY 7 DECEMBER — Romans 12:11 (LB)

Working like Jesus

Never be lazy in your work but serve the Lord enthusiastically.

Life seemed to have gone badly wrong for Amanda. She'd always wanted to be a missionary, but when she met her husband at Bible college she decided to settle for being a pastor's wife. Somehow he never made the grade, and now he worked in a biscuit factory. Amanda was fed up, overweight and stuck at home with three children. She couldn't even find a role at church because of her husband's awkward shifts. The house was a tip and somewhere under all the mess she had mislaid her joy.

'You know what, God,' she said belligerently one night when the baby had earache. 'All I wanted to do was serve you! I would have gone anywhere in the whole world, put up with anything, and worked round the clock, but you landed me in this dump doing absolutely nothing!'

Isn't it strange how God seems to meet us at our lowest moments? Amanda was giving the baby yet another drink when she suddenly felt the Lord was speaking to her. 'You are giving this cold water to me. You serve me by serving your family and I want you to know I appreciate the way you care for me.' Amanda's tears splashed down onto the baby's head as she began to see her life from a totally new perspective.

It is easy to admire people who do exciting things for God while we plod on in a boring job or care for elderly (or very young) relatives. Yet, surely, serving the Lord full-time means doing the next small job for him—whether that means preaching to thousands or comforting one baby. To Jesus it is not what we do that counts but *how* we do it—and *who* we do it *for*. His aim was to please his Father in everything he ever said or did and I'm sure that applied when he tidied the carpenter's shop or raised the dead and preached the sermon on the mount.

Lord, show me how to work for you today, and help me give it my best shot. Amen.

JRL

TUESDAY 8 DECEMBER   Romans 12:12 (LB)

Rejoicing like Jesus

Be glad for all God is planning for you. Be patient in trouble.

When my six children were small I was taken seriously ill, and for the next eight years I was trapped in a wheelchair. Life was extremely tough and sometimes I just did not want to go on living. The pain and frustration of that illness seemed so ghastly at the time, but now when I look back I can see how much good God was able to bring to me and my family through that experience. I also guess that when I look back after a few billion years in heaven, those difficult years will seem like a few brief unpleasant seconds in comparison with all the fun I'll be having.

We don't tend to look at our problem-dominated lives from the perspective of eternity. Heaven, however good it's going to be, seems a long way ahead when we feel ill, can't pay the bills or we've lost someone we loved dearly. Yet Paul tells us to fix our attention on the future and be glad because of all the good things God is planning. I think he is talking about this life, as well as heaven. Earlier in this same letter he says that God wants to bring good out of all the nasty things which hit those of us who love him and are willing to fit into his plans (Romans 8:28).

A few years after Paul wrote this letter to the Christians in Rome, their Emperor, Nero, went mad. He began throwing them to his lions or burning them alive to light the city streets at night. I guess they must have remembered what Paul told them in today's verse because it was the patient, even joyful, way that they died which impressed so many people that Christianity spread even more rapidly around the Roman Empire.

'Let us fix our eyes on Jesus, the author and perfecter of our faith, who for the joy set before him endured the cross, scorning its shame, and sat down at the right hand of the throne of God' (Hebrews 12:2, NIV).

JRL

WEDNESDAY 9 DECEMBER *Romans 12:12 (LB)*

Praying like Jesus

Be prayerful always.

I used to get mad with Paul for saying we should 'pray without ceasing'. He obviously didn't have six children! Yet it does seem as if Jesus, in spite of his pressured lifestyle, was in continuous contact with God, as well as spending those early mornings alone with him (Mark 1:35). But is it possible in our modern world to 'be prayerful always'?

Obviously, talking to God in words all the time is impossible. People in the office or supermarket would think we were nutty and we simply wouldn't cope if we didn't keep our minds on the job. I think I'm beginning to realize that prayer is a relationship which doesn't depend on words. Perhaps when the person you love most is always there with you, you get so close that words lose their importance. You just love them through everything you do, say or think.

We all know we need to spend a few moments each day 'plugging into God', but it's vital not to sign off with a final 'Amen'. We need to stay in his presence as the day unfolds, acknowledging that he is there by wordlessly referring everything to him. When the phone rings I don't say, 'Almighty Father, please assist me to communicate appropriately during this conversation.' My heart simply sends a 'help' in his direction as I lift the receiver. When I'm hoovering, or driving to work, my thoughts are all over the place, but I keep reminding myself to bring God into them. I'm not asking for anything, I just share what I'm thinking.

Whenever I get the nagging feeling I've fouled up, and need his forgiveness, I don't wait until my next official prayer session to sort it out, because I loathe feeling out of sync with him.

Sharing the little enjoyments of each day is important too—new buds on a house plant or the rich taste of the soup I'm cooking.

Lord, my days are just a string of small actions, leading on from one another. Show me how to keep on invoking your presence as I move through each of them. Amen.

JRL

THURSDAY 10 DECEMBER   *Romans 12:14, 17a, 20a (LB)*

Reacting like Jesus

If someone mistreats you because you are a Christian, don't curse him; pray that God will bless him ... Never pay back evil for evil ... Instead, feed your enemy if he is hungry, if he is thirsty give him something to drink and you will be 'heaping coals of fire on his head'.

We all know this is how Jesus behaved. When people yelled abuse at him, he kept quiet; he even healed one of the thugs who arrested him. But what about us? I think it's humanly impossible to love and treat kindly someone who has abused you, deserted you or ruined your life. Forgiving is too tough on our own—we need God's help. All he needs is our willingness to spit out the hate and, in its place, breathe in his love and forgiving grace. I find I have to do that *every time* the bad memories come back into my mind. Perhaps I'll have to keep at it for the rest of my life.

Julie's daughter was traumatized when a neighbour exposed himself in the park. For three years Julie couldn't look out of her front windows in case she saw this man who lived opposite. 'But I had my revenge,' she said. 'I kept bringing the subject up in conversations with my neighbours, working them up against him until no one would speak to him—or his wife.'

Then Julie became a Christian and after a talk on forgiveness she made the decision to try it, 'so long as I never have to speak to him'. One day his wife was taken ill, and he went to see her in hospital each evening after work, returning late and tired. Julie kept feeling God wanted her to plate up an extra meal at supper-time, and take it over to him when he returned. The very idea revolted her, but the night she finally managed it, he thanked her with tears pouring down his face. They both knew it was much more than a plate of supper.

Lord, forgive me that I can't forgive, but I want to want you to make me willing. Amen.

JRL

FRIDAY 11 DECEMBER *Romans 12:19, 21 (LB)*

Forgiving like Jesus

Never avenge yourselves. Leave that to God, for he has said that he will repay those who deserve it. [Don't take the law into your own hands.] ... Don't let evil get the upper hand but conquer evil by doing good.

Once, in my wheelchair days, one of my sons behaved so badly I wished I could get up and commit murder, but I was helpless. I could only say, 'You just wait till your father comes home.' God isn't a sentimental old grandpa, beaming indulgently down on the world. He gets violently angry when one of us (whom he calls the apple of his eye) is hurt by someone else. Hell-fire was not a medieval invention; Jesus often talked about it. If hell and punishment didn't exist, then there would have been no need for him to die on the cross. Of course we don't like the subject, but the Bible tells us just as much about God's wrath as it does about his compassion.

If he simply patted the heads of people who selfishly destroy others, and let them off, it would be impossible for us ever to forgive. We would feel it was our responsibility to make them suffer, but knowing we can leave their punishment to God on judgment day sets us free from the obligation. The trouble is, we *want* to pay them back ourselves so that we can see them squirm. It is that kind of vengeful anger that destroys us, and we have to bring it to God for his forgiveness, or we're in danger of forfeiting our own forgiveness and also facing God's wrath (Matthew 6:15).

Have you ever thought what a ghastly punishment God might have planned for those heartless soldiers who banged nails through his son's hands, laughing at his agony? Hell would be too good for them. But we may meet them all in heaven one day, simply because Jesus prayed for them. 'Father, forgive them,' meant, 'Father, let them off.' Forgiving is one thing, but praying that God will also forgive goes far beyond that—it could set them free from punishment.

Are you willing to forgive as Jesus forgave?

JRL

Saturday 12 December — Romans 12:15, 18 (LB)

Feeling like Jesus

When others are happy, be happy with them. If they are sad, share their sorrow ... Don't quarrel with anyone. Be at peace with everyone, so far as it depends on you.

Empathy is not like sympathy which feels *for* others. Empathy takes us right inside someone else and feels the pain *with* them. It understands because it identifies, but it isn't just an emotion—it does something positive to help. Jesus cried for Mary when her brother died, but he did more than weep—he raised him from the dead. Jesus could have stayed in heaven, feeling sad for the mess we're in, but he felt strongly enough to come and do something about it.

Feeling like Jesus means more than just listening to someone's problems after church and then saying a quick prayer and telling them to keep smiling. It means identifying so completely you know instinctively what practical help they and their family will need during the coming week—and then giving it.

Pippa never went to church and was too shy to make friends. At first she did not know her neighbour Carol was a Christian—she just thought she looked nice. One day, without warning, Pippa's husband left her with three children. She was so shocked she took an overdose. As she came round in hospital she saw Carol's face.

'Don't worry about the kids,' Carol said, 'I've got them round at my place. And when you're better I'd love you to come and stay, too, for a bit.' Over the next weeks Pippa felt totally surrounded by the love and care of Carol's church. Suddenly she had the friends she had always wanted and it wasn't long before she met Jesus himself.

He must sometimes look down at desperately sad people like Pippa and long to help and comfort them—but how can he, unless one of us acts for him?

Lord, I want to feel the same about people as you do. Send me out into the world which you love, and let me be so like you that people will be drawn to your love which fills my heart. Amen.

JRL

SUNDAY 13 DECEMBER *Isaiah 11:1 (NIV)*

New growth from old stumps

A shoot will come up from the stump of Jesse; from his roots a Branch will bear fruit.

It was an impressive storm. Lightning. Thunder. Wild, blowing rain. A deafening crack and a one hundred-year-old cedar crashed to the ground across the street. The next day the groundspeople came and sawed a clean cut through the ragged break of that once majestic tree trunk. Now it's a stump. Ring after ring of golden-brown yearly growth graced that sliced, rugged trunk stump. Reflecting past greatness, but now felled. All visible signs of life gone.

The stump of Jesse is that which was left of the great nation of Israel, descendants of King David, son of Jesse. By the time Isaiah is speaking, there is not much that is mighty or majestic of the once glorious nation of Israel, now felled by God for her faithlessness. Little left indicating life, and definitely no fruit. Simply a stump.

But in this passage we have God promising through Isaiah the prophet that from that dead and decaying stump of Jesse, a shoot will spring forth that will bring fruit. It is foretelling of Jesus being born into that historic family tree of David, son of Jesse.

But how long must Israel wait for this new shoot? Young saplings started to grow from the once great tree across my street the following summer. A short wait for new life. Israel waited much longer. But finally, Jesus came bringing new life and new hope and new possibilities—the fruit of his presence.

But what about the stumps of our lives? What life potential is hidden underneath the growth rings on our stumps? Are they simply wrinkles of time or do they hold the promise of future grace?

Dear Jesus, you know the stumps in my life. Stumps from a power surge of lightning. Stumps from the gardener's saw. Stumps from my own destructiveness. Felled life. Places of deadness. But still, I am rooted in you, source of life. Bring new, fresh shoots from my stumps. Produce your fruit in me.

EP

MONDAY 14 DECEMBER   *Isaiah 11:2–3 (NIV)*

The Spirit resting

The Spirit of the Lord will rest on him—the Spirit of wisdom and of understanding, the Spirit of counsel and of power, the Spirit of knowledge and of the fear of the Lord—and he will delight in the fear of the Lord.

She was so little. Her little bottom just fitted in my cupped hand. She curved warmly over my breast and snuggled quietly. Completely relaxed. She fitted perfectly there. Resting. It's funny but some things just fit together, don't they? Like my baby daughter on my breast.

In reading these verses I get the same feeling about the Spirit of the Lord just fitting 'him'—resting on Jesus. He who is the new shoot growing out of the stump of Jesse. Just as my baby daughter curved over my curves and rested, the two of us, perfectly sized for one another, so the Spirit of the Lord rests and curves on 'him'. Quietly resting, not struggling or striving, simply resting.

God gifts Jesus with the Spirit of wisdom and of understanding. That gift of seeing the heart of issues and the heart of people. Of knowing the human experience. Gifting him with the Spirit of counsel and of power. That gift of strategy, of being able to sort things out, of deciding the right thing to do in a situation. And having the power to do it. He will have the Spirit of knowledge and fear of the Lord. That gift of knowing the Lord. Of really grasping what life and living and God are all about. And being able to live it.

Jesus, shoot of Jesse, resting in the Spirit of the Lord—a perfect gift.

'I keep asking that the God of our Lord Jesus Christ, the glorious Father, may give you the Spirit of wisdom and revelation, so that you may know him better. I pray also that the eyes of your heart may be enlightened in order that you may know the hope to which he has called you, the riches of his glorious inheritance in the saints, and his incomparably great power for us who believe' (Ephesians 1:17–19).

EP

TUESDAY 15 DECEMBER *Isaiah 11:3 (NIV)*

Fearful delight

And he will delight in the fear of the Lord.

What a delightfully contradictory verse: 'He will delight in the fear of the Lord.' Do you very often combine delight and fear? Stop for a minute and reflect on these two phrases. What comes to mind? And who comes to mind?

Are you chuckling to yourself as you are remembering the fun you used to have with Aunt Sidney and her eccentric, warm-hearted ways? And remembering a respectful distance with her. A distance, a respect, a something that told you 'never, never, be rude to her'.

When I think of delight, I think of the face of a child as she peers at the wonder of the Christmas tree ablaze with lights. Or the response of a child when she shares a joke with an adult and knows they laugh together. Funny how I associate delight with children. Delight seems to be a childlike quality. It has to do with wonder and awe. It has to do with that ability to be unselfconscious, abandoning oneself to the moment.

Do you remember in C.S. Lewis' *The Lion, the Witch and the Wardrobe* when Susan, in dialogue with Mr and Mrs Beaver, asks if Aslan is 'safe'? Mr Beaver's astonished response is, 'Safe? Who said anything about safe? 'Course he isn't safe. But he's good. He's the King, I tell you.' Susan experiences this wonderful mixture of delightful romps with Aslan and fearful awe in his kingly presence. Aslan is good and he is scary.

We struggle to hold such different feelings together. We quickly adjust our feelings or our circumstances so we have only one feeling at a time. But this dulls the rich fabric of relationships. Our relationship with God will invariably be complex and at times scary.

Jesus, you know that we are often fearful when we collide with your scariness. Teach us how to dance with the vibrant rhythms of our delight in you and of our fear of you. And how to bring these together that we may delight in our fear of you.

EP

WEDNESDAY 16 DECEMBER Isaiah 11:3 (NIV)

Oh God, you know

He will not judge by what he sees with his eyes, or decide by what he hears with his ears.

They were an impressive family. The parents were both successful healthcare professionals, very active in the church and local community. Their three children were all successful university students.

One of their daughters sat across from me weeping in pain as her story spilled out. Her father had sexually abused her throughout her childhood. This was the first time in twenty-two years that she had told anyone her story. The father, after hearing his daughter's disclosure, denied the possibility of abuse and suggested, 'She always had emotional problems.'

To look at this family on Sunday at church was to see a wonderful, nice-looking family. Jesus will not judge by what is seen or what is heard, but rather by his own knowing and understanding. By his grace the truth was disclosed in this family.

We naturally judge by what we see with our eyes and decide by what we hear with our ears. I wonder what Jesus sees when he looks at you and me and I wonder what he knows? His ears might hear your voice singing his praise in the church choir but he might recognize your words of heartless gossip spoken about your neighbour. He might see your cheerful service to the elderly and he might see your cruelty to your own daughter.

It is for these things that he came: to challenge and expose the truth of our own double standards and to transform us. To know when we are sorry and to forgive us. He also came to bless the good that we do and are. To know the deep inside and give comfort to its cruel wounds. To know our weakness and to strengthen us. He sees and he hears. And he knows.

Lord, have mercy. Heal our woundedness.
Christ, have mercy. Cleanse us of the wickedness within us.
Lord, have mercy. Release us to delight in our relationship with you.

EP

THURSDAY 17 DECEMBER   *Isaiah 11:4 (NIV)*

Can we really judge the needy?

But with righteousness he will judge the needy, with justice he will give decisions for the poor of the earth.

What on earth does judging the needy mean? Giving just decisions for the poor, that seems fairly clear. But judging the needy… are we allowed to do that?

I remember a woman coming into our church office asking for help. She had a young child who was sick and her welfare cheque had been spent. Could we please give her money to pay for some medications for her child. We did.

The next day we received a phone call from both the local police and three neighbouring churches saying that this woman, in fact, had no child and had been to every 'soft touch' in the community. I was really furious. Ripped off by a con artist! I was angry because I had been 'sucked in'. And then I felt stupid and angry, and very uncharitable towards 'the needy'.

How can we tell who is needy and who isn't, who is genuine and who is ripping us off? Well, we can't! We can maybe get smarter in the ways in which we help and support the needy and the poor but the Christian mandate is clear: we are to care for the poor and the needy. That is not optional for a Christian.

As I have read and reread this verse I have been encouraged because the 'shoot of Jesse' will judge her actions—and my reactions. He will judge fairly and equitably. He will give just decisions for the poor. A justice that will not tolerate injustice by the needy or the self-sufficient. A justice that will not favour the poor or the wealthy, the wicked or the con artists.

Jesus will not judge by what he sees with his eyes, or decide by what he hears with his ears, but with righteousness he will judge the needy, and with justice he will give decisions for the poor of the earth. He will judge with a perfect balance of mercy and justice.

Dear God, give us the gift of grace to hold mercy and justice in balance.
EP

FRIDAY 18 DECEMBER   Isaiah 11:4 (NIV)

We wait in hope

He will strike the earth with the rod of his mouth; with the breath of his lips he will slay the wicked.

These words have energy and power in them: striking the earth and slaying the wicked. Puts the fear of God in you, doesn't it?

A part of me wants to shout, 'Yes. Down with the wicked. Be done with evil.' But am I allowed to want the wicked removed? In fact, to be slain? I don't know about you but I am weary, soul-weary, of the wicked. I have received too many stories in my office about cruel and senseless abuse. Too many stories of evil winning. I am fed up with watching yet another news story on TV of yet another senseless massacre.

And somewhere, somehow, I have this idea that as a Christian I am not supposed to get passionate about the elimination of the wicked and evil. Now I am not talking about everyday wickedness such as self-centredness or our pathetic little prides, but I am talking about that intentional, calculated wickedness that attacks innocent and vulnerable people in our society, those who have no defence.

I can imagine the breath that breathed life into Adam and Eve. And the breath that breathed the Holy Spirit upon the disciples in John 20:21. And I can imagine the same breath on the same lips slaying the wicked. I can imagine the anger of God on the wicked. But am I allowed these imaginings? I'm not sure, but I long for Jesus to come and bring justice and righteousness. To have our world conform to his will—on earth as it is in heaven.

This verse holds an action of the future. For our earth is still cursed and the wicked still flourish. And we still wait. We wait in hope for Jesus to return again to earth to release us from the battle with evil. We wait for the promised restoration and justice. We wait for evil to be removed.

O Lord Jesus, come quickly. You know we are weary in our battle with evil. Keep us faithful. Give us the strength to hold on to hope.

EP

SATURDAY 19 DECEMBER — Isaiah 11:5 (NIV)

Designer clothing

Righteousness will be his belt and faithfulness the sash around his waist.

While doing my internship as a counselling psychologist, I was instructed on what to wear to *look professional*. Standard suit and blouse were expected. I sometimes wondered if wearing blue jeans and hiking-boots might not have been more symbolic of my willingness to walk alongside my clients, and therefore maybe more professional. When my husband became an Anglican priest, our daughters took great joy in giggling at their father's 'dresses'. It was quite a change from the usual blue jeans and trainers of his previous youthwork job.

We often know something about people by what they wear. The robes of a priest. The uniform of the Salvation Army on skid row. The strange headgear of bishops. The tattered clothing of the 'bagladies' of our urban streets. The conformity of 'alternative clothing'. The body-piercing jewellery of our teenagers. Such clothing tells us something about the person wearing the garments. Something about who they belong to, who they associate with and what purposes they commit themselves to. So it is in this verse: righteousness will be his belt and faithfulness the sash around his waist. These are inherent qualities of Jesus, the 'shoot of Jesse'. In the Old Testament, the belt symbolizes a willing readiness to act. In this case, acting in righteousness and faithfulness. Actions that will reflect the purposes of God for a people he loves.

Stop and reflect for a moment. What clothing are you known for? What garments would you like to add to your wardrobe? Listen to what Paul says to the Colossian Christians in chapter 3:

Every item of your new way of life is custom-made by the Creator, with his label on it. All the old fashions are now obsolete … So, chosen by God for this new life of love, dress in the wardrobe God picked out for you: compassion, kindness, humility, quiet strength, discipline … And regardless of what else you put on, wear love. It's your basic, all-purpose garment. Never be without it.
THE MESSAGE

EP

SUNDAY 20 DECEMBER *Isaiah 11:6–7 (NIV)*

Radical change coming

The wolf will live with the lamb, the leopard will lie down with the goat, the calf and the lion and the yearling together; and a little child will lead them. The cow will feed with the bear, their young will lie down together, and the lion will eat straw like the ox. The infant will play near the hole of the cobra, and the young child put his hand into the viper's nest.

When the Messiah returns for the second time, the whole of nature itself will be transformed. The old relationships of hunter–hunted, victor–victim that were necessary to maintain life will be done away with. The wolf that preyed on the lamb for food; the leopard that ripped apart the goat for nourishment; the lion that tore at the calf and the yearling to feed its young. They will lie down and live together and new relationships will take their place.

The cow and the bear, with their young, will feed together and lie down together without threat to their young alongside the lion eating straw like the ox. There will be a return to the feeding habits and relationships of the garden of Eden, changing the very nature of these creatures. A little child, leading the wolf and the lamb along with the leopard and the lion, will not only be safe in their company but will assume leadership in guiding them to rest and reconciliation. And a helpless infant will play safely beside a cobra's nest, breaking that old enmity between serpent and humanity and abolishing Eden's curse.

It is almost impossible to imagine such changes and such reversals of nature as this. It is almost impossible to imagine that Jesus is able to bring such newness to relationships and to earth. Yet he will.

Dear Jesus, give us a gift of hope to believe that you will come again. A gift of hope to believe that you have the will and the power to bring about such a new earth as this. Give us hope as we live in our present broken world. Give us perseverance to wait in faith.

EP

MONDAY 21 DECEMBER Isaiah 11:9 (NIV)

Fragrant gifts

They will neither harm nor destroy on all my holy mountain, for the earth will be full of the knowledge of the Lord as the waters cover the sea.

I loved going to visit her. She always seemed so glad to see me; so warm and inviting. She reminded me of fresh bread coming out of the oven: fragrant, good and wholesome. Her face radiated a joy that held me spellbound. Her eyes would pull me in and hug me. I felt enveloped in a cloud of goodness in her presence—as if I had come home. I would experience a deep quiet at the same time as being more energized and more alive than in other places.

She was a mentor to me. At the same time, she seemed to enjoy me as much as I enjoyed her. She had the spirit of the knowledge of the Lord. And she nourished me with that knowledge.

As my mentor's spirit filled her home and her relationships, so the Lord's knowledge will fill his home, his holy mountain, and draw us in—in fear and delight. Then we will be filled with the knowledge of the Lord. When Jesus returns we will know him and be known by him.

Those forces and those things that have had such power to destroy and wound will have no power or access to destroy and harm again. The 'shoot of Jesse' will see to that. He will reign with righteousness and rule with justice. And all tears shall be wiped away. For we will have come home. We will belong as we have never belonged before. And we will delight in God as much as he delights in us. As the waters fill the seas to capacity, so the knowledge of the Lord will fill us, and the whole earth, to capacity.

Dear Jesus, release us to delight in the fragrance of your presence here on earth while we wait for your coming to take us home. And let the responses of our hearts, our minds and our bodies be a pleasing, fragrant gift to you.

EP

TUESDAY 22 DECEMBER   Luke 1:26–38 (GNB)

Preparation

God sent the angel Gabriel to a town in Galilee...

As we face the last few frenzied days of preparation I am amazed at how often I hear people say, 'Wouldn't it be nice to get back to how it was at the first Christmas?'

Because of course there wasn't one! A first Christmas, I mean. When it really happened it wasn't a festival for people to take part in. It wasn't a story which began with the angel Gabriel and finished with the magi. It was a chunk of real life—their life. Not so very different from the lives of so many children of God from Adam onwards. There were always miracles and angels and glory shining from just around the corner, but there was invariably the bleak bit first where there didn't seem to be hide nor hair of a miracle to be seen. Then the people involved were given the chance to be part of the never-ending story just for a page or two. On Mary's page she is asked to say 'yes' to God's request that she should carry his Son in her womb without a single promise of protection. Because she agreed, the next chapter could begin.

When Windsor Castle was damaged by fire in 1992 there was little hope that it might be restored to anything like its former glory. In fact it is now more beautiful than ever, but there is one bit that isn't a replica of the original. In honour of the heroism shown on that night there is a new stained-glass window depicting the firefighters in action, now an integral part of the castle's story.

As we approach Christmas this year let us take time to look at what might be asked of us as bit players in the ever-unfolding drama of the history of God's children. What will we allow to be written on our page? What will be in our stained-glass window? Let's hope it's not just a picture of us stuffing our faces with mince pies!

Dear Father, this Christmas please give us a job to do for you. And help us to do it.

BP

WEDNESDAY 23 DECEMBER Matthew 1:18–25 (GNB)

Joseph did what was right

Mary was engaged to Joseph, but before they were married, she found that she was going to have a baby by the Holy Spirit. Joseph was a man who always did what was right, but he did not want to disgrace Mary publicly; so…

Cuckold. Throughout literature there have been great tragedies which centre on the husband who has reason to believe he has been cuckolded. Othello is just one of many. The only good thing that could possibly come out of the ghastly situation was that everyone was bound to be on your side, egging you on to seek revenge in whatever way was fashionable at the time.

Times have changed. With growing equality of women evening out the odds against who will be betrayed, and increased indulgence towards extra-marital affairs generally, stoning is hardly considered an acceptable form of revenge. One thing hasn't changed. There will still be an outraged support group urging you to punish the one who deserved to 'get what was coming to him or her'.

It didn't help then and it doesn't now.

Forgiveness of those who have done us wrong is never popular with those who love being a verse in a hymn of hate. But we are asked by the same Lord who was at that time nothing but a fingertip in size, to forgive seven times seven, and then again. Laying down the weapon of righteous anger is a lonely decision, frequently misunderstood and despised. Believing in someone against all the odds takes a courage few of us are asked for. But Joseph was.

And us? Is there someone whom we need to begin to forgive? Someone whom we have every right to be deeply angry with, even someone who has caused our lives never to be the same again, someone who is, in fact (unlike Mary), guilty as sin?

Dear Father, this one is really hard. Help us please to want to begin to set free the person or the memory of the person who has most hurt us. Pour over and into us your beautiful sparkling waterfall of forgiveness so that this Christmas we can begin to be a channel of your peace.

BP

THURSDAY 24 DECEMBER   Luke 2:1–6 (GNB)

Make room

Joseph went from the town of Nazareth in Galilee to the town of Bethlehem in Judea...

There is one period in my life that I never want to repeat. I was a first-year student at Bristol University, living in digs miles away from the centre with no evening bus service. I had made next-to-no friends and became so appallingly unhappy that it hurt like a hunger. At its worst I took to carrying my begging bowl of loneliness from one of my fellow students' lodgings to another, hoping for some scraps of conversation and companionship which could act as a temporary substitute for the food of friendship I craved.

There are certain times when being alone is particularly foul, aren't there? Times when it seems impossible to believe that there is no visible sign of the gaping wound of loneliness. And it's worse in a crowd, especially a crowd surging towards a common goal, oblivious of everything except their desire to get there.

Many friends who live on their own tell me that it is not Christmas Day itself that is worst, although that can be very hard. It is the period leading up to it when everyone else is complaining of the cost and the exhaustion, and you are not penniless or tired because you have no expensive presents to buy and no hoards to feed.

This Christmas, if we are lonely, let us for once break our rules and acknowledge our need to be part of the turmoil, the mince pie making, the 'wishing it was all over'. If we are busily involved in all that turmoil, let us open our door, acknowledge our need, and let someone into our muddles of preparation. Let us not make anyone stand outside our friendship and have to knock. We need each other.

Dear Father, we remember Mary and Joseph, exhausted and in pain in a town where there was no room for them, and where everyone else was preoccupied. Even if we find it hard naturally to open our door, or to enter someone else's, let us do it this Christmas, in memory of them.

BP

FRIDAY 25 DECEMBER (CHRISTMAS DAY)   *Luke 2:7 (GNB)*

God with us

She gave birth to her first son, wrapped him in strips of cloth and laid him in a manger—there was no room for them to stay in the inn.

Why do we want this night to be silent and holy? Why are we so determined to separate our spiritual experiences from the marketplace of life? I'm sure that Jesus was born with all the pain and struggle of my first child. It probably took hours and hours. The greatest miracle of all slithered messily out to be held with all the tearful tenderness of exhausted, joyful new parents throughout the ages. His first bleating cry would have probably been drowned by the noise and confusion outside in the streets of Bethlehem, overflowing as it was with visitors there to take part in the census. The pervading smell would not have been of incense, the vehicles bringing the crowds being of the four-legged variety, and there would have been hundreds of them. Struggles in high places were happening as the new king, Herod, tried to consolidate his position. There was corruption and crippling taxation under the new Caesar. That very night people would have died. Other babies would have been born. There would have been robberies and rapes.

But we don't like it. We want to shut out reality and wait for the magic of Christmas to start. No wonder we get disappointed!

Let us try to make this Christmas Day different. Let us simply live it to the full, trying to welcome everything that happens, good and bad, as part of our celebration of God coming to be right inside the chaos with us.

Dear Father, you loved us so much that you gave your only son to treat in any way we wished. Fill us with the knowledge of that wondrous truth today, Father. Help us to give ourselves to you now, knowing that you will not throw fairy-dust over our day to create an advertiser's dream sequence, but that you will transfigure our hearts so that those closest to us catch a glimpse of your presence and understand a little of the meaning of Emmanuel, God with us.

BP

SATURDAY 26 DECEMBER *Luke 2:8–20 (GNB)*

The shepherds

There were some shepherds in that part of the country who were spending the night in the fields, taking care of their flocks...

Why do the shepherds always get such a demeaning press? 'How wonderful that the lowly (substitute "thick") shepherds are the baby's first visitors.'

In pre-industrial, rural Britain I think there would have been far more understanding of the type of person we are talking about. Shepherds had to be loyal, tough, hard-working, brave and often quick-witted professionals. Jesus, the very baby they were called upon to visit, called himself a shepherd and drew a comparison between the dedication of the good shepherd and the hired man who would run from the wolf because he was not prepared to risk being killed for the sake of someone else's sheep.

So what interests me is not that they were lacking in formal education, but that they left their sheep to 'go now even unto Bethlehem to see this thing which had come to pass'. We are not given to understand that there were any angelic promises about sheep-sitting or wolf sedation and it would have been not only more than their job was worth but also against their principles to abandon the sheep in their protection. Yet they did.

What are we to make of this? That it's all right to leave our defenceless children in the house and go off to Midnight Communion? Of course not! But there may be something that is so ingrained into us as being the right and proper thing to do at Christmas, that our eyes and ears are closed to the possibility of a divine special call on our time and energies. I may be the very person God has chosen to step outside my conventional behaviour just this once to do a special job for him. What a thought!

Dear Father, can you please help us to listen to you very carefully today? Is there something you want us to do for you? Someone you want us to see or to listen to?

BP

SUNDAY 27 DECEMBER Matthew 2:1–12 (GNB)

Journeying on

Some men who studied the stars came from the East to Jerusalem... [The star] went ahead of them until it stopped over the place where the child was.

One of the glorious truths I have learned as an adult, but which seemed to elude me as a child, is that being wise does not automatically mean being sensible. As a child I knew that being wise meant putting on your vest in winter and not patting strange dogs. The magi were wise and probably usually sensible as well, but not this time. This time they followed that part of their learning which said, 'I think this is really important. I really think we should do this', against all common sense.

Do you, like me, have a few glorious, technicoloured memories from your childhood of when something wonderfully exciting and out of the ordinary happened to you? I can still see the lights on Llandudno pier sparkling like Las Vegas while I walked, clutching my parents' hands, up late on holiday and about to be allowed for the first and probably only time to eat fish and chips out of a newspaper!

For my own children I had thought, sadly, that it would take more than that to create a magic-carpet memory that would never fade, but when I asked my older boys what they remembered most from their childhood, it was a car journey that we made through the night to go on holiday in Cornwall in the winter. They were crammed into their sleeping bags, lying on top of the cases in the back of the car, staying awake all night singing songs, listening to tapes and munching sweets. Unheard-of forbidden pleasures! We don't remember it *quite* as rosily as they do but I know that the cosiness and excitement and feeling of adventure is something they will never forget.

Dear Father, as we look towards a new year, help us to allow for the possibility that you may have an adventure for us, a journey to make into unknown territory either in real terms or in our thinking and feeling.

BP

MONDAY 28 DECEMBER   Matthew 2:12–14 (GNB)

Deliverance

They returned to their country by another road, since God had warned them in a dream not to go back to Herod. After they had left, an angel of the Lord appeared in a dream to Joseph...

Just about everything in God's book is topsy-turvy, isn't it? Just when we have seen that the wise men behaved apparently foolishly, we see God and his angels behaving with a common sense that is very down to earth!

The magi had agreed to return to Herod to tell him where the new king of the Jews had been born. Clearly they were not such good readers of character as they were readers of the stars, and it needed the direct intervention of God in a dream to prevent them doing something very silly indeed. Soon after that, angels appeared in another dream, giving Joseph very direct orders to escape with his wife and child while the going was good. Can we assume from this that there are times when it is right to use our common sense and put ourselves and our safety first? I do hope so.

I do know that there have been times in my adult life when I have longed to be given permission by a grown-up to take a safer road out of a confrontational or demanding situation; times when I have known that I am spiritually and emotionally run down or out of my depth and need to be excused from life for a moment.

Jesus taught us to ask his Father daily to 'lead us not into temptation and deliver us from evil'. So I think it must be OK to trust that, though he certainly never wants us to opt out of difficult situations, he will be pleased to see us using his gift of common sense once in a while.

Dear Father, we really need to take the prayer that your Son gave us more seriously, don't we? Please deliver us from evil today and help us to use your gift of common sense to keep ourselves safe and free from temptation.

BP

TUESDAY 29 DECEMBER   *Matthew 2:16–19 (GNB)*
Bethlehem and Dunblane

When Herod realized that the visitors from the east had tricked him, he was furious. He gave orders to kill all the boys in Bethlehem...

Fifteen small girls stood tensely to attention on stage, tiny feet turned out, smiles bravely in place, eyes shining with excitement, waiting to be marked for the solo festival dances they had been practising for months and had just performed. One by one, fifteen little would-be ballerinas' faces crumpled as the adjudicator tore their efforts to pieces.

'That woman is evil,' whispered my friend as she tearfully watched her little daughter bewilderedly struggling to retain her frail dignity in the face of this extraordinary attack. Bit of an exaggeration, but, yes—evil, the capacity to snuff out the light, extinguish hope, to destroy and enjoy doing it.

In an age when even the behaviour of Regan and Goneril, King Lear's horrendous daughters, can be portrayed as stemming from childhood problems, and when parenting and society are blamed in equal proportions, it is unfashionable to talk of absolute evil. With a background in childcare I am one of those who finds it hard not to look for excuses for antisocial behaviour, but I am increasingly sure that Satan must be chortling at our attempts to excuse evil.

Children being subjected to inappropriate sexual experiences of any sort and, even more horrifically, tossed away like broken toys afterwards, is evil directly influenced by the evil one.

When the darling, shiny-eyed offspring of loving parents are wiped out by madmen, whether in Dunblane or Bethlehem, that is undiluted evil, evil too poisonous for us to fight in our own strength, but fight we must, and spiritual battles need spiritual weapons.

Dear Father, we fall on our knees before you, begging forgiveness for the evil in our land. We know that, too often, we have tried to fight evil in our own puny strength. Help us now and in the future to stand in the light and battle to keep the light alive in our children's eyes.

BP

WEDNESDAY 30 DECEMBER
John 1:1–5 (NRSV)

The light that shines

What has come into being in him was life, and the life was the light of all people.

We have a friend who, for several years, was the curate of a small Anglican church in one of the roughest areas in the East End of London. Sunday services took place in a run-down community hall in the centre of the estate. The windows only remained in place because of barbed wire bunched around them. The outside walls were smothered with graffiti. As their first Christmas approached, he worried that he might not be able to create any sense of the specialness of the festival. Then he had an idea. He bought every little candle he could lay his hands on, and on Christmas Eve placed them in every safe spot he could find in the hall. When his little congregation arrived for the midnight service they were speechless on seeing their drab hall sparkling with what must have seemed a million little lights. It proved to be a wonderful Christmas. Not only did they experience the truth of these words of John in a dramatically visual way, but they also felt special because of the effort our friend had made.

The light that came into the world was the flame of the living God, dangerous as well as beautiful, revealing and destroying evil, intent on casting out darkness. It was also warming and healing, easing pain, lessening the coldness of loneliness and despair. It was enhancing and attracting. Everyone who met Jesus wanted to be close to him and many felt that they too could be whole, better people for the experience. What a challenge for us who have been called to be light and salt!

Dear Father, help us to remember that it was not so much what you said or did but who you were that attracted people to you and made them feel so much better. Please work in us in whatever way you think necessary so that when people meet us they can see your light shining powerfully through our graffiti-covered outer selves.

BP

THURSDAY 31 DECEMBER   *John 1:5–14 (NRSV)*
Living lights

The light shines in the darkness and the darkness did not overcome it.

Jesus passed on the responsibility of being light in the world to us. Knowing how difficult that would be for such feeble creatures, he offered the gift of his light in the form of the Holy Spirit to any who asked for it.

We once visited some incredible caves in New Zealand. Herded into rowing-boats outside, we were then steered slowly underground for a short distance, lit by electricity. Suddenly our guide turned off the lights and we found ourselves in a wonderland, sparkling lights transforming the dank stone walls into a heavenly canopy. The roof was smothered with millions of minuscule glow-worms whose living phosphorus illuminated our eerie journey through the watery underworld.

Being light to the world does not mean that we merely speak words of light or point people to the light but that we allow the glory of the Holy Spirit within us to stab the darkness of our dank world and transfigure it.

If we choose, we can be a link in the chain of minuscule living lights that has been shining since he left this world. Sometimes there is a gap in this extraordinary time-line where the forces of darkness appear to have snuffed out the lights in a particular area of the world. Amazingly, in most of these places the lights have rekindled themselves, rather like those novelty birthday candles that refuse to be extinguished.

Last year, at the funeral of Princess Diana, the song *Candle in the Wind*, originally written in tribute to Marilyn Monroe, became, with a few subtle changes, a world symbol for the tragic snuffing out of a legendary life before its time.

Jesus is not a legend living on after his flame has died. He lives. Through us his light continues to bring life and love to our world. Surely, if it was going to go out it would have done so by now!

Dear Father, today we ask for courage to offer ourselves truly as living light in whichever area you choose.

BP

DAY BY DAY WITH GOD

MAGAZINE SECTION

November 135
Living stones 136
Being a list-maker 141
Lighten our darkness! 144
On the way to Bethlehem 148

Other Christina Press titles 152
Other BRF titles 154

Order forms 156

Subscription information 158

Woman Alive – monthly £1.80

Essential reading for every christian woman – offering guidance and support, Woman Alive is everything a woman's magazine should be, plus much more!

My Life – Published twice yearly – this high quality magazine is designed to help christian women everywhere share the good news of Jesus Christ! Ideal for outreach! (25 copies – only £8!)

FREE SAMPLE COPIES!

Please send me a free sample copy of
☐ Woman Alive
☐ My Life

Name ....

Address ....

.... Post code ....

Return to – Sue Mills, Christian Media Centre (DBD)
96 Dominion Road, Worthing, West Sussex BN14 8JP

November

Mary Reid

Dear Lord,

The trees were beautiful this morning.
Most of the leaves have fallen
And the bare branches were a misty brown,
Their golden leaves trodden underfoot.
Yet even today
When winter waits to pounce,
When skies are grey
And spring seems far away,
We live in hope.

Show me Lord how to live today.
Just give me your love today.
Let me shed my coat of cares and confusion
And rest in your love.
If I can do that today
Then who knows
What we can achieve
Tomorrow.

The leaves are fallen, dead and gone,
But the tree is not dead.
Tomorrow it will grow new leaves,
Fresh and green—and more than this year.
It had to die a little in order to grow.
Do we do that, Lord?

Living stones
Elaine Pountney

You also, like living stones, are being built into a spiritual house (1 Peter 2:5, NIV).

The cold arctic wind was whipping our legs as we stood in the snowy barrenness of a January day on a downtown street in Montreal. My husband, Michael, was ecstatic: 'Let's kneel down right here on the sidewalk, Elaine, and thank God!' My feeble, apprehensive and somewhat bewildered response was: 'I'll stand and pray. I can't kneel.' So as the pedestrians strode past us, we prayed. No, Michael prayed, thanking God for sending him to this new church: Bishop's Missionary to the Church of the Ascension.

The church was an ugly, sombre, red-brick, fortress-like, somewhat decrepit structure. On the south side of the church was a dark oppressive nightclub. On the north, a pool hall. Across the street and down a bit, a porn theatre with a twenty-foot high neon sign of a nude woman.

Inside, the church was beautiful, with some of the most impressive wood craftsmanship I had ever seen in a church. At the front, just above the altar, was a superb wooden carving of a lamb immediately below a magnificent stained-glass window of Jesus as shepherd. Those two images are still vivid in my mind's eye.

On our first Sunday there, in a building that could easily seat six hundred people, eighteen of us gathered, average age sixty-seven, to proceed through the deadliest sung Communion service I have ever experienced. As I sat there that first Sunday with our young daughters, I was curious to know how these ruins would be rebuilt, restored and renewed. This place of worship needed more living stones.

The task was immediately obvious: both the physical structure and the community of believers required rebuilding. The physical structure, ancient by Canadian standards, was built in the late 1800s. You were never sure, upon entering the building, whether you would be privileged to a hot shower as yet another hot-water pipe exploded, or be called upon to pull on the wellies and activate the sump pump to subdue rising waters in the basement.

Rebuilding begins

Both my husband and I agreed that God would have to move in remarkable ways to rebuild this once thriving Montreal anglophone parish. Clearly, this church had to become a church of the surrounding neighbourhood—only two of the eighteen parishioners lived within walking distance. So I left my job as a research associate in cardiology and opened a shop-front community centre—almost next door to the barber shop. L'Ascentre, as it was called, served a nutritious lunch and sold used clothing very cheaply. And the people of the neighbourhood began to come.

Speaking only Spanish, the new Mexican bride of one of my colleagues from the lab where I had worked came and made the first pots of soup for us—delicious fish soup. Although an atheist, she was happy to be a part of the project. Muslim students from Morocco regularly came and joined us for lunch. These students missed home, family and community. Somehow this funny little shop-front centre had the aroma of home. And that intangible thing that connects people to one another began to happen. The Breath of Life was breathing life into us—and the dead stones began to live.

The conversations around the lunch tables were wonderful. 'Why are you doing this?' 'What on earth could motivate you to do this?' The people of the neighbourhood began to be curious about this thing that was happening. 'I've never even noticed there was a church across the street before. I've walked by it every day for years. What is this church thing anyway?' And together we talked about what this thing called church was. 'You really believe in this Jesus person?'

Two women, twins, in their sixties, salt of the earth, loved coming to L' Ascentre. They were as wide as they were high and full of fun. Both of them had learning disabilities, and as children they were sent to a religious school. In tears, one of these women recalled that if she could not recite her arithmetic tables and do the calculations correctly, the teacher would take her and set her in a tub of cold water until she could remember. Slowly these twins learned to trust us and began to come to church. About a year later one of them was confirmed. She brought a contagious joy of Jesus into our community of believers—a real gift to us. Another living stone.

A short, bent-over woman who looked like she was eighty-one crept into L'Ascentre one day. She slowly backed her way around the walls of our centre. Just looking and checking us out. She came back for a whole week doing exactly the same thing. Then I put her to work serving soup and sandwiches. She loved it. Several months later she came to me, agitated, and wanting to talk. She asked if I would teach her how to write her name. We agreed that every morning, fifteen minutes before the centre opened, I would teach her how to write. I will never forget the day she came in, absolutely glowing because she had learned to write her name. She began to stand taller and straighter. She even started to smile, comb her hair and wear lipstick. It turned out that she was fifty-one and had eleven children, most of whom we eventually met. She, her husband and two of her children joined us—and the church grew.

And Sam, dear 37-year-old Sam. He was about six foot five inches tall, wore a black bowler hat, always wore a suit, and always carried an umbrella. He used to come every day for lunch; he enjoyed the goodness of the place as we laughed, cried and worked with one another. Sam loved coming to L'Ascentre but never shook my hand when he arrived, unlike others who would say, 'Hi', shake my hand or give me a hug in greeting. Then he explained he was an orthodox Jew. And I was a woman.

One day I commented that he always looked so smart in his suit and hat and I asked him if he ever dressed any differently. His comment was: 'My mother won't let me out of the house unless I'm dressed like this!' We chuckled together. One day Sam came in after a few days' absence. I told him that we had missed him. He said that he had taken two bottles of aspirin and had been admitted to the psychiatric ward of a local hospital. We all listened. I wondered what God was thinking of our conversation that day in L'Ascentre. It felt as though God was smiling in love for Sam as he was sheltered and cared for among our living stones.

Changed lives

It was our habit to start our work day by praying and reading a part of the New Testament together. Usually there would be about eight of us there. One day we read the story of the good Samaritan and started talking about it. Someone asked if the people who walked by the bleeding and wounded man would be forgiven. This conversation triggered something deep within these broken people. We soon had a heated discussion going. Frank, a gigantic 65-year-old, started pounding the table with his fist, refusing to forgive his mother who had repeatedly tried to abort him during her pregnancy or for giving him away to an uncle when he was four. Jack, an ex-drug dealer, meanwhile was loudly shouting that he was not prepared to forgive any jerk who had ripped him off. The two elderly twins were visibly shaking in terror at what was happening. No one had prepared me to lead this kind of a Bible discussion. I did the only thing I knew would work. I said, 'Let's pray.' Frank and Jack sat down, the women looked relieved, the others continued in their frozen state. At the end of my prayer, Frank prayed, 'Elaine says we should forgive so I'm going to try.' Jack muttered, 'Me too.' And our day continued from there in its usual way. But the lives of Frank and Jack had changed. It's as if something broke and released them into a new place of freedom. They changed. New life in old stones.

After that, Jack started bringing some of his buddies to our Wednesday night meetings of prayer and praise at the church. Usually about twelve of us would meet, including some of those wonderful original eighteen parishioners. But we ran into a bit of a dilemma. Jack's buddies came carrying their hardware. Out of the top of their boots we could see their guns and their knives. But, hey, they kept coming and kept participating.

Later we added a few micro-industries to the centre to create employment in our neighbourhood. After donations of several sewing-machines, we began to teach sewing as a marketable skill. We started by sewing teddy bears. Huge Frank started making teddy bears. Even with the neurological damage caused by his mother's attempts to abort him, Frank was able to sew teddy bears. He was our most enthusiastic teddy bear maker. Teddy bears transformed his life. He named his first teddy bear and loved it with a gentleness none of us knew was inside him. He went on to make nine, all loved and valued. He began to enjoy going home to his one-room apartment because his teddy bear was there to greet him, taking the loneliness out of his home. All the love and gentleness inside found a focus and an expression and he became a living stone building us up.

Then we added a printing press micro-industry and a bookbindery. The printer was a rotund, white-bearded, Father Christmas-like, chuckling man who was regularly used by film companies as an extra simply for his appearance. He was the messiest printer I have ever met but a big-hearted person. The book-bindery was operated by two very talented women. Both were mystified how they had come to be involved with a Christ-centred church. But they loved the sense of community, and they leaned on living stones, drawing strength.

Community and change

Our community kept growing and developing. We started having parish suppers which became wonderfully chaotic events filled with laughter and warmth where our elegant original eighteen welcomed the latest Franks and Jacks. We worked hard together painting and scrubbing and cleaning and repairing the church. The building itself had a heartbeat again.

We began as a church to get involved with cleaning up the neighbourhood. So together with the wider community we joined in marches protesting about the pornography theatre, wanting to make our neighbourhood a suitable and safe place to bring up children. In fact, many changes occurred in the neighbourhood because of the collective vision. And our church community was an important aspect of these changes. Even the neighbourhood recognized that the church was alive again. As we became a community we began to know who we were as the church of Jesus Christ—and richly hued we were: anglophone, francophone, Ugandan, Greek, Chinese, East Indian, Tamil, employed, street people, truck drivers, single mums, rejected kids, wards of the state. It was wonderful. Everyone belonged and everyone had a place. Our Sunday services resembled a United Nations gathering.

That is not to say that this was an easy place in which to be living and working. But it was definitely good. People were being healed and community was happening. And in our church Jesus Christ was worshipped. And known. God was building our community with living stones. The pipes still regularly burst and the basement still flooded but God was rebuilding and restoring through these living stones.

But God's ways are not our ways. Today, ten years later, that church is a city library. No longer a building of worship. The bricks and mortar may crumble and disappear, but the people, these living stones, are still God's people being built into a spiritual house in many different places. Part of the larger, permanent, eternal Church of Jesus Christ.

Being a list-maker

Margaret Killingray

Are you a list-maker? If you are, then read on and, as one list-maker to another, we may learn some truths about ourselves. If you aren't then please read this, because you almost certainly have one in your immediate circle of family and friends, and we do need to be understood.

Making lists is my way of controlling my world. If I have written down what I have to do today, then I am halfway to doing them, even if they never get done! I heard of one person who began their list with 'Get up, have breakfast', because they had such a feeling of achievement when they could cross these off the list pretty early on. This would not have worked for my children when they were teenagers, I have to say. (I very much admired the woman I met years ago whose list at the time was headed by 'Have a baby'. She was very pregnant, so it wasn't wishful thinking.)

Differences

We are all so very different in the way we do things. Some of us may have filled in those self-revealing questionnaires that appear in magazines: *Find out whether you are a good listener; How good are you at attracting the opposite sex; Do you wear the trousers or are you a doormat?* These are often simple and not very accurate versions of the kinds of personality tests that are used for business executives, and working teams, so that they can see why they do not function together very well.

Sometimes, at the Institute for Contemporary Christianity where I work, when we are running courses on how to live and work together as Christians we give everyone a page of circles—about the size of an old penny, with twenty on the page, and ask everyone to do something with them. Most people then say, 'Do what?' And we say, 'Anything.' Some people immediately begin to fill in the circles systematically, beginning from the top left-hand corner and moving down as you would a page of writing—English writing, that is. They may do the same thing with each circle—I have one sheet in front of me where every circle is a clock face showing a different time; another has filled in the inside of every circle with something different—the back of an elephant, a plate with food on it, two circles made into a bicycle, etc. Some time later others begin to doodle, joining the circles up with lines, writing a message in them; or just scribbling. If people have not done such an exercise before, they can be totally amazed that all their fellow participants have not automatically filled the circles in the same way as they have. What seemed the obvious way to them was not obvious to the others.

Priorities

List-makers tend to be the ones who begin at the beginning and work systematically through the page. They know order when they see it, and find disorder difficult to cope with. As a list-maker personality, I am pretty near neurotic about tidiness. My children say that I cleared up their toys while they were still playing with them. If the house was on fire, they tell me I would write a list of priorities for rescue before I could act.

I have to admit, and you may be the same, that as a list-maker personality, I have difficulty in actually doing the things that are on the list. This means that there are areas of my life as a Christian which I find difficult. I can happily talk about praying; list the old patterns for prayer—ACTS: adoration, confession, thanksgiving, supplication, etc. I can explain why we should pray; explain the gospel passages which show us Jesus at prayer. *But* I have to force myself to actually pray! I have lists of people and things to pray for, but once they are down on the list, a quick skim down them and I can tick them off for the day. To spend time praying about them, thinking about them, listening to God as I hold them in my mind, *seems* like a waste of time.

I am happy with an orderly system for Bible reading, giving the passages to read for each day. But I never give myself enough time to read the passage properly—as long as there are five minutes to read it quickly so that I can tick it off the list, then I'm away. I find passages like Psalm 119, which seem to be saying the same thing over and over again, hard to deal with. I'm impatient in church, because I've done it already—this morning, last week.

God's plan

Jesus stopped on his way to heal Jairus' daughter, to love and affirm the woman who had bled for twelve years. Jesus went away to pray all night, and was interrupted by people who wanted to be with him and talk to him; he didn't turn them away. The good Samaritan certainly had to scrap his list on the way to Jericho. Perhaps the others who 'passed by on the other side' were list-makers. God has a plan—a list, even—for the salvation of the world, and he waits patiently for his people to turn to him, loving them and weeping over them, and when they get it wrong he rejigs the list. Perhaps Martha was a list-maker. Mary was certainly on her rota for the washing-up, and that was more important than listening to Jesus, for her. Perhaps Judas was a list-maker, and he may have wanted Jesus to lead the Jews to victory here and now, and he couldn't change his mind.

If you are a list-maker, then know yourself and recognize your problems; be prepared for the Holy Spirit to change you and change your lists, however painfully. But also be aware of your strengths; flexibility is a gift of God, but so is order and pattern. Non-list-makers, you may be missing important steps in your walk with the Lord because you are being spontaneous and reacting to the present. We all need each other, encouraging each other, and sometimes admonishing each other. In our prayer groups, in our close Christian friendships, understanding our different personalities can liberate us to be ourselves with each other and with God.

Lighten our darkness!

Christine Leonard

It's run-up-to-Christmas time again and my heart sinks from that moment in late August when the cellophaned puddings and pictures of Santa start appearing in the shops. Once the festival gets underway I enjoy the times with friends and family, the church services, the food and drink, the fairy lights strung from fir trees swaying gently against a frosty sky. But, during November and December as the hype increases and the days grow ever darker, so my gloom deepens. It happens every year and the other day I was asking God why.

We were spending a few days of the autumn half-term holiday in northern France, pottering around ancient walled towns and strolling along coastal paths, enjoying spectacular views in the clear, cool air. Before returning home, we decided to visit the vast Cité Europe, near the French entrance to the Channel Tunnel. Describing itself as the 'ultimate shopping centre', it boasts a massive hypermarket, 11 major stores, 150 smaller specialist boutiques, a 12-screen cinema and a mock village made up of every kind of eating place—all under one roof.

Visiting the hypermarket

Car parks surround this monolith on both sides and two levels—room for half the world to park, you might think, yet we nosed our way round, negotiating our way through vehicles parked in all the wrong places, and were about to give up when we spotted someone backing out of a space. We parked there, right next to Tesco Vin Plus, in whose entrance we found a crowd of shoppers with empty trolleys. A Tesco employee barred the way in. They do that in some of our English supermarkets just before Christmas, something to do with safety limits. We decided to try the hypermarket instead.

We were allowed in this time, but the first aisle, though extraordinarily wide, had jammed solid in an impassable tangle of trolleys through which people were attempting to push and squeeze their way. Very few managed to get close enough to read the labels on the wine bottles, let alone to pick one up. I don't suffer from claustrophobia but something like panic began to surface in me.

It reminded me of the fish which, years ago, had frightened my children. Huge and dark, they splashed and writhed in the shallows of the ornamental lake the moment we started throwing bread for the ducks. Tails and fins lashed against the others in a feeding frenzy. Their mouths gaped wide and ugly in air, not water. They seemed alien, because they did not glide, calm and graceful like other fish we had seen. Long after the ducks had eaten their fill, the mass of carp still fought over scraps of stale bread.

But this human feeding frenzy felt far more alien and frightening than the fish. 'Let's get out of here,' I said. My husband and daughter nodded agreement. We turned tail and almost ran back to the car park, then drove away from that place as fast as we could.

The crush had been made up mainly of British people out to beat the tax man, most French being at lunch at the time. My husband, speeding away from that hypermarket, said the whole thing felt immoral and I knew what he meant. Most of the British people had come over on day trips and this was all they would see of a beautiful land. It wasn't quite like the Vikings' rape and pillage because the French owners obviously welcomed the money, but still a raid mentality existed and it felt tainted, like prostitution.

Christmas consumerism

Seeing rampant consumerism exposed for the ugly thing it was, I understood why I feel so depressed each year before Christmas, as crowds pack the supermarkets, pushing trolleys loaded with far more than the largest of families could possibly eat before the food perishes. While a few may entertain hordes, surely those who are being entertained need to shop less, so everything should even out. But it never does!

My neighbour saw a man die in our local supermarket the other year, right in front of the delicatessen counter. Apparently these pre-Christmas shopping deaths are relatively common, because stress levels soar so high. People aren't designed to live like this; it isn't sane behaviour, any more than our French experience was, and it depresses me because suddenly civilization seems very thin. People who for much of the year seem reasonably kind and decent individuals become driven by naked greed. This consumerism seems such an empty god, our ever-larger shopping temples such soulless places to worship. I think I feel depressed because, more than at any other time, I see that so many around me are truly lost—and I feel helpless to do anything about it.

On the ferry back to England I sat reading *Angels Keep Watch* by Carol Hathorne (Christina Press, 1997). Carol writes vividly about Kenyan Christians who remain cheerful through some appalling conditions and make their requests known to God with great confidence. These are not requests for baubles and luxuries but matters of life and death, as when someone needs urgent medical attention but has no money to pay for it. These same Christians, who have almost nothing, give away the little they have, again and again, as a natural part of their worship and utter trust in Jesus.

Carol's account gripped me, but every now and then I glanced up from the page to see fellow passengers struggling along with yet more crates of beer from the duty-free shop on board. There were special deals on tickets and I've never seen a ferry so full. People were sitting on stairs, on corridor floors, so many people. They seemed like sheep without a shepherd, on one level unimaginably rich, yet by the standards of those Kenyan Christians, so poor. Children grizzled and adults looked exhausted, unhappy. I wished I could do something, but what? Stand up and preach? I'd have been stopped even if I'd had the nerve in the first place. I felt helpless and hopeless. I didn't even know what to pray. These people were strangers to me but I wondered how God must feel, loving each one, hurting for them, while so few ever wanted to know him.

Light in a dark place

Next day I was talking to God about this when I found myself thinking about the room where we had stayed in France. A black blind which pulled down over its single dormer window ran in grooves at the sides, efficiently blocking all light except for a centimetre at the bottom. We stayed deep in the country and in the middle of the night the room remained utterly without light. All I could see was that centimetre-wide strip at the bottom of the window, about a metre long, brushed by the faintest of starlight. Then, well before dawn, I started to see the outline of the rest of the window, then faint shapes of the furniture and the angles of the ceiling. Finally, through that tiny gap, there poured enough light to read by.

It doesn't take very much to light a dark place and just the merest glimmer can reveal enough for people to see that there is more to their world than they had realized. Jesus came as a light into our world on that first Christmas. John tells us that his life was the light of men and that the darkness has not overcome it. The window helped me see that light really is far stronger than darkness. As Christmas approaches and people mill about in the gloom, predatory as those fish, I know I should pray that the light of Jesus will shine through some gap in their defences and then grow, as inevitably as the dawn lit that dark bedroom.

I know that I should pray that God's light will indeed shine through, and then be creative in lighting a few candles myself. I know also that I am not very good at that and so this has become my prayer:

> *Father God, please help me to keep my eyes focused on your brightness. I know how much I need your help if my hands are to stay bold and ready to light candles from your fire and then pass them on to others. I've glimpsed a little of your heartbreak and your brilliance too. Help me to live so that I make a difference for you in this world. Amen.*

On the way to Bethehem

An extract

Hilary McDowell

The latest book from popular *New Daylight* and *Day by Day with God* contributor Hilary McDowell is BRF's Advent book for 1998, *On the Way to Bethlehem*. It aims to take the reader on a spiritual journey of discovery, putting the wonder back into a season so often burdened by pressures of work, money, gift-buying, or family relationships.

Hilary uses the well-loved BRF pattern of daily Bible readings, together with a passage of comment and a point for reflection or a prayer. But by combining well-known Advent scriptures with Bible passages less commonly associated with this time of year, she has written a particularly fresh and imaginative series of readings in her own unique style.

As she herself puts it: 'In search of the Christ child we leave the familiar and travel expectantly, open to the possibility of God surprising us along the way. The destination is God's choosing, the itinerary etched by the Bible, the search is for Jesus.'

Hilary is a well-known author and all-round communicator, as well as a Presbyterian deaconess, despite coping with numerous disabilities since birth. She has also written *Some Day I'm Going to Fly* (Triangle, 1995) and *Around the World on Eighty Prayers* (Triangle, 1997).

The following extract presents a day's reading from the first section of *On the Way to Bethlehem*, entitled 'Packing the Case'.

Section 1: Packing the case

The decision to journey
Read Genesis 1:1–3. 'Let there be light.'

A choice lay ahead. The traveller could allow herself to be dragged towards Bethlehem, this year, kicking and screaming through the tinsel-laden pressures of the expected route to Christmas. Already her local radio station had been announcing the countdown of the days even before the leaves had started to fall. Was the world getting crazier, or was it just her?

Would she journey or not? All around her, folk were expressing the desire to stay at home, lock all doors, put the phone off the hook and 'opt out' of the pandemonium. After all, hadn't she 'been there, bought the T-shirt', year after year?

On the other hand, suppose she hadn't seen it all? Supposing God could surprise her? What if there was something at the destination more than shopping aisles and carols and mince pies?

She was already fed up with the shortening, dark, old days before Christmas, with their impending sanity-free workload of preparation, the anticipation of reaching the new year with a deep desire to lie in a darkened room until spring. There was altogether too much darkness, in more ways than one.

Yes, she would go. Right from Genesis he had promised light, and she owed it to herself to make the journey. What she dreaded was packing the case.

Drag the luggage from below the bed and set it out for a good airing—slightly musty from months of disuse. Will it be big enough to hold all the necessaries? Let's see—she selected the most favourite clothes, the ones that made her feel and look the best. Then in went the protection from the sun, protection from cold, and lots of underwear.

Better not be caught out financially, she thought. Cheque book, cash, identification for border crossings, and passport. Extra insurance for loss of luggage, time, personal injury, just in case. Followed by maps, instructions, repair kit, first-aid box. An expanding bag or two would not go amiss, and the hold-all and shopping bag and…

What a weight to carry, she thought, but kept stacking. She packed for the weather she expected, the enjoyment she craved, the 'image' to be created. Of course the emotional and psychological baggage packed itself automatically. It was all in there, past experiences and learned strategies. Fears from yesterday's wounds and failures, bad memories and good ones.

GENESIS 37:1–4

Jacob dwelt in the land of his father's sojournings, in the land of Canaan. This is the history of the family of Jacob.

Joseph, being seventeen years old, was shepherding the flock with his brothers; he was a lad with the sons of Bilhah and Zilpah, his father's wives; and Joseph brought an ill report of them to their father. Now Israel loved Joseph more than any other of his children, because he was the son of his old age; and he made him a long robe with sleeves. But when his brothers saw that their father loved him more than all his brothers, they hated him, and could not speak peaceably to him.

Joseph gathered a heavy burden of luggage early in life. A favourite child with the privileges and the jealousies that come with such a position. A spoilt child with a great deal more than a many-coloured coat, but the coat didn't help the situation as such a garment, in the culture of the day, denoted a favour which was normally the right of the eldest son. Then, to add insult to injury, the favouritism nurtured in him arrogance, detestable to his brothers. At seventeen, he was 'sneaking' to his father about their behaviour. His journey of life burdened him early with some very heavy luggage indeed.

Traveller, as we step out towards Bethlehem this year, it's good to take time to examine what is packed in the old suitcase. Items hidden there from years of hurts and wounds and jealousies and anger and unforgiveness. We need to cleanse our expectations of the journey, open ourselves to God's itinerary, relinquish our 'image' of ourselves, whether that be good or bad. Joseph wasn't planning to go anywhere; as far as he was concerned, he'd arrived! Will our traveller begin her Advent journey making the same mistake?

Dear God,

It's hard to prepare for the journey with a fresh spirit. Been here before, we think. Father, ruffle my packing enough to help me see the vision you have for me along the way.

Please gift me with the right amount of wonder for anticipation, a healthy degree of trepidation to know I travel in the hands of a living God who can touch my yesterdays as much as my tomorrows. Lord, make me expectant, make me new. Amen

An extract from *On the Way to Bethlehem* by Hilary McDowell, published by the Bible Reading Fellowship. Available from Christian bookshops everywhere, or in case of difficulty direct from the Publisher using the order form on page 157.

Other Christina Press titles

Who'd Plant a Church? Diana Archer
£5.99 in UK
Planting an Anglican church from scratch, with a team of four—two adults and two children—is an unusual adventure even in these days. Diana Archer is a Felixstowe vicar's wife who gives a distinctive perspective on parish life.

'An extremely gifted writer.' *Jennifer Rees Larcombe*

Dear God, It's Me, and It's Urgent Marion Stroud
£6.99 in UK
The beauty of depth of these prayers, covering every aspect of a woman's life, make them unforgettable. Topics range from A *Bride's Prayer* for the eve of her wedding to A *Prayer for Ironing*, *Shopping with a Daughter* and *Feeling Unwanted*. Each double page meditation is enriched with scripture and well-chosen quotations.

Precious to God Sarah Bowen
£5.99 in UK
Two young people, delighted to be starting a family, have their expectations shattered by the arrival of a handicapped child. And yet this is only the first of many difficulties to be faced. What was initially a tragedy is, through faith, transformed into a story of inspiration, hope and spiritual enrichment.

'I was deeply moved by Sarah's story. Do read it.' *Celia Bowring*

Angels Keep Watch Carol Hathorne
£5.99 in UK
A true adventure showing how God still directs our lives, not with wind, earthquake or fire, but by the still small voice.

'Go to Africa.' The Lord had been saying it for over forty years. At last, Carol Hathorne had obeyed, going out to Kenya with her husband. On the eastern side of Nairobi, where tourists never go, they came face to face with dangers, hardships and poverty on a daily basis, but experienced the joy of learning that Christianity is still growing in God's world.

God's Catalyst Rosemary Green
£8.99 in UK
The highly commended guide to prayer counselling.

Rosemary Green's international counselling ministry has prayer and listening to God at its heart. Changed lives and rekindled faith testify to God's healing power. Here she provides insight, inspiration and advice for both counsellors and concerned Christians who long to be channels of God's Spirit to help those in need.

God's Catalyst is a unique tool for the non-specialist counsellor; for the pastor who has no training; for the Christian who wants to come alongside hurting friends.

'To read this book will be helpful to any Christian interested in helping others.' *John White*

Women Celebrating Faith Lucinda S. McDowell
£5.99 in UK
In this challenging and gripping collection, women from all walks of life take time to look back on their lives at forty and reflect on the spiritual lessons they've learned. No matter what your age you will be encouraged by the experiences of these women.

'A book that makes you look forward to mid-life.' *Susan Yates*

Life Path Luci Shaw
£5.99 in UK
Personal and spiritual growth through journal writing. Life has a way of slipping out of the back door while we're not looking. Keeping a journal can bring it all back. Luci Shaw shows how to do it and how it can help us grow in our walk with God.

'A delight.' *Madeleine L'Engle*

Pathway Through Grief edited by Jean Watson
£6.99
Ten Christians, each bereaved, share their experience of loss. Frank and sensitive accounts offering comfort and reassurance to those recently bereaved. Jean Watson lost her own husband 18 months ago. She believes those involved in counselling will also gain new insights from these honest personal chronicles.

All the above titles are available from Christian bookshops everywhere, or in case of difficulty direct from Christina Press using the order form on page 156.

Other Bible Reading Fellowship titles

A Feast for Advent Delia Smith
Reflections on Christmas for every day in Advent
£5.99 in UK
Delia Smith, Britain's best-selling and much loved cookery writer, shares her own insights on preparing for Christmas and on the Christmas story itself. With printed Bible passages, comments, prayers and meditations. Royalties from this book go to the Quidenham Children's Hospice.

Following the Saints Heather Butler
£2.99 in UK
Provides young readers with a fun way to count down the days of Advent. There are saintly stories on every page: historical saints who loved God; biblical saints who helped spread the good news about Jesus; and some who were friends of Jesus when he lived on earth. Every page has puzzles, prayers and things to think about as you count down the days and follow the saints to Christmas.

Learning the Language of Prayer Joyce Huggett
£6.99 in UK
Through Bible readings, reflections and exercises, Joyce Huggett looks at several aspects of prayer. Relevant both to beginners and those looking to deepen their prayer life. Full colour throughout.
   'Yet again, Joyce Huggett seems to have her finger on the spiritual pulse.' *Mary Ridgewell, The Lee Abbey Fellowship.*

Heartfelt Gerrit Scott Dawson
Finding our way back to God
£3.99 in UK
An exploration of ten episodes from the Gospels which will take you into the presence of Jesus to allow him to touch your life. This book is for people who are looking for a stronger connection with God, who feel that their experience of traditional faith has not been enough for them and want to rediscover their first love for him. With questions and reflection exercises.

The Ultimate Holiday Club Guide Alan Charter and John Hardwick

Book £9.99 in UK
Cassette £5.99 inc. VAT in UK

An ideas-packed guide to running holiday clubs from two authors who are both very experienced in the field. All the material has been thoroughly field tested in holiday clubs around the country. Just add a pinch of planning, a dash of enthusiasm and bring to the boil! Contains themes for three complete programmes with ideas for warm-ups, songs, sketches, quizzes, games, crafts and Bible narrations. Includes musical score for all the songs used in the book and photocopy permission for fun-sheets. Also gives advice on planning and preparation. Material can also be used in children's clubs/after-school and Sunday programmes.

The cassette includes theme songs and memory verses to accompany all three themes. This cassette can be used to play during your club, as a learning resource if you are planning to use your own musicians, or to have available for the children to take away with them as a memento of their holiday club experience.

Barnabas Discovers Christmas Taffy Davies
£2.99 in UK

Barnabas thought he knew quite a lot about Christmas. He knew how busy the children were as they prepared for their Christmas play in the village school, and he could play some of the carols they sang, on his horn.

But the thing Barnabas knew best was that it was the time of year when everyone gave him presents. For Barnabas, this was the real meaning of Christmas. But he was about to learn something very special about Christmas that he hadn't realized before...

The first in BRF's Bible Days with Barnabas series for 6–8 year olds, with puzzles and pictures to colour on every page as you follow the adventures of Barnabas the little school bus.

All the above titles are available from Christian bookshops everywhere, or in case of difficulty, direct from BRF using the order form on page 157.

Christina Press Publications Order Form

All of these publications are available from Christian bookshops everywhere, or in case of difficulty direct from the publisher. Please make your selection below, complete the payment details and send your order with payment as appropriate to:

Christina Press Ltd
Highland House
Aviemore Road
Crowborough
East Sussex
TN6 1QX

		Qty	Price	Total
8704	Life Path	___	£5.99	___
8705	Pathway Through Grief	___	£6.99	___
8706	Who'd Plant a Church	___	£5.99	___
8707	Dear God, It's Me, and It's Urgent	___	£6.99	___
8702	Precious to God	___	£5.99	___
8703	Angels Keep Watch	___	£5.99	___
8700	God's Catalyst	___	£8.99	___
8701	Women Celebrating Faith	___	£5.99	___

POSTAGE AND PACKING CHARGES				
order value	UK	Europe	Surface	Air Mail
£6.99 & under	£1.25	£2.25	£2.25	£3.50
£7.00–£14.99	£3.00	£3.50	£4.50	£6.50
£15.00–£29.99	£4.00	£5.50	£7.50	£11.00
£30.00 & over	free	prices on request		

Total cost of books £ _____
Postage and Packing £ _____
TOTAL £ _____

All prices are correct at time of going to press, are subject to the prevailing rate of VAT and may be subject to change without prior warning.

Name _____
Address _____
_____
_____ Postcode _____

Total enclosed £ _____ (cheques should be made payable to 'Christina Press Ltd')

☐ Please send me further information about Christina Press publications

DBDWG0398

BRF Publications Order Form

All of these publications are available from Christian bookshops everywhere, or in case of difficulty direct from the publisher. Please make your selection below, complete the payment details and send your order with payment as appropriate to:

BRF, Peter's Way, Sandy Lane West, Oxford OX4 5HG

		Qty	Price	Total
016	On the Way to Bethlehem		£5.99	
3519	A Feast for Advent		£5.99	
015	Following the Saints		£2.99	
3080	Heartfelt		£3.99	
3555	Barnabas Discovers Christmas		£2.99	
2974	Learning the Language of Prayer		£6.99	
3286	The Ultimate Holiday Club Guide		£9.99	
2985	The Ultimate Holiday Club Cassette		£5.99	

POSTAGE AND PACKING CHARGES				
order value	UK	Europe	Surface	Air Mail
£6.99 & under	£1.25	£2.25	£2.25	£3.50
£7.00–£14.99	£3.00	£3.50	£4.50	£6.50
£15.00–£29.99	£4.00	£5.50	£7.50	£11.00
£30.00 & over	free	prices on request		

Total cost of books £ _____
Postage and Packing £ _____
TOTAL £ _____

All prices are correct at time of going to press, are subject to the prevailing rate of VAT and may be subject to change without prior warning.

Name _____
Address _____

_____ Postcode _____

Total enclosed £ _____ (cheques should be made payable to 'BRF')
Payment by: cheque ❏ postal order ❏ Visa ❏ Mastercard ❏ Switch ❏

Card no. ☐☐☐☐ ☐☐☐☐ ☐☐☐☐ ☐☐☐☐

Card expiry date ☐☐☐ Issue number (Switch) ☐☐☐

Signature _____
(essential if paying by credit/Switch card)

☐ Please send me further information about BRF publications

DBDWG0398   The Bible Reading Fellowship is a Registered Charity

Subscription information

Each issue of *Day by Day with God* is available from Christian bookshops everywhere. Copies may also be available through your church Book Agent or from the person who distributes Bible reading notes in your church.

Alternatively you may obtain *Day by Day with God* on subscription direct from the Publishers. There are two kinds of subscription:

Individual Subscriptions are for four copies or less, and include postage and packing. To order an annual Individual Subscription please complete the details on page 160 and send the coupon with payment to BRF in Oxford. You can also use the form to order a Gift Subscription for a friend.

Group Subscriptions are for five copies or more, sent to one address, and are supplied post free. Group Subscriptions run from 1 May to 30 April each year and are invoiced annually. To order a Group Subscription please complete the details opposite and send the coupon to BRF in Oxford. You will receive an invoice with the first issue of notes.

All subscription enquiries should be directed to:

BRF
Peter's Way
Sandy Lane West
Oxford
OX4 5HG

Tel: 01865 748227
Fax: 01865 773150
E-mail: subscriptions@brf.org.uk.

Group Subscriptions

The Group Subscription rate for Day by Day with God will be £9.00 per person until April 1999.

☐ I would like to take out a group subscription for _____ (Qty) copies.

☐ Please start my order with the January/May/September* 1999 issue
I would like to pay annually/receive an invoice with each edition of the notes*. (*Please delete as appropriate)

Please do not send any money with your order. Send your order to BRF and we will send you an invoice. The Group Subscription year is from May to April. If you start your Group in the middle of a subscription year we will invoice you for the remaining number of issues left in that year.

Name and address of the person organising the Group:

Name_____
Address _____
_____
_____
Postcode _____ Telephone _____
Church _____ Name of Minister _____

Name and address of the person paying the invoice if the invoice needs to be sent directly to them:

Name_____
Address _____
_____
_____
Postcode _____ Telephone _____

Please send your coupon to:

BRF
Peter's Way
Sandy Lane West
Oxford
OX4 5HG

DBDWG0398   The Bible Reading Fellowship is a Registered Charity

Individual Subscriptions

☐ I would like to give a gift subscription (please complete both name and address sections below)

☐ I would like to take out a subscription myself (complete name and address details only once)

The completed coupon should be sent with appropriate payment to BRF. Alternatively, please write to us quoting your name, address, the subscription you would like for either yourself or a friend (with their name and address), the start date and credit card number, expiry date and signature if paying by credit card.

Gift subscription name _____
Gift subscription address _____
_____
_____ Postcode_____

Please send to the above for one year, beginning with the January/May/September 1999 issue:

	UK	Surface	Air Mail
Day by Day with God	☐ £10.50	☐ £11.50	☐ £14.00

Please complete the payment details below and send your coupon, with appropriate payment, to **The Bible Reading Fellowship, Peter's Way, Sandy Lane West, Oxford OX4 5HG.**

Your name _____
Your address _____
_____
_____ Postcode_____

Total enclosed £ _____ (cheques should be made payable to 'BRF')
Payment by: cheque ☐ postal order ☐ Visa ☐ Mastercard ☐ Switch ☐

Card no. ☐☐☐☐ ☐☐☐☐ ☐☐☐☐ ☐☐☐☐

Card expiry date ☐☐☐☐   Issue number (Switch) ☐☐☐

Signature _____
(essential if paying by credit/Switch card)

NB: These notes are also available from Christian bookshops everywhere.

DBDWG0398   The Bible Reading Fellowship is a Registered Charity